ABOUT KUMON

What is Kumon?

Kumon is the world's largest supplemental education provider and a leader in producing outstanding results. After-school programs in math and reading at Kumon Centers around the globe have been helping children succeed for 50 years.

Kumon Workbooks represent just a fraction of our complete curriculum of preschool-to-college-level material assigned at Kumon Centers under the supervision of trained Kumon Instructors.

The Kumon Method enables each child to progress successfully by practicing material until concepts are mastered and advancing in small, manageable increments. Instructors carefully assign materials and pace advancement according to the strengths and needs of each individual student.

Students usually attend a Kumon Center twice a week and practice at home the other five days. Assignments take about twenty minutes.

Kumon helps students of all ages and abilities master the basics, improve concentration and study habits, and build confidence.

How did Kumon begin?

IT ALL BEGAN IN JAPAN 50 YEARS AGO when a parent and teacher named Toru Kumon found a way to help his son Takeshi do better in school. At the prompting of his wife, he created a series of short assignments that his son could complete successfully in less than 20 minutes a day and that would ultimately make high school math easy. Because each was just a bit more challenging than the last, Takeshi was able to master the skills and gain the confidence to keep advancing.

This unique self-learning method was so successful that Toru's son was able to do calculus by the time he was in the sixth grade. Understanding the value of good reading comprehension, Mr. Kumon then developed a reading program employing the same method. His programs are the basis and inspiration of those offered at Kumon Centers today under the expert guidance of professional Kumon Instructors.

Mr. Toru Kumon
Founder of Kumon

What can Kumon do for my child?

Kumon is geared to children of all ages and skill levels. Whether you want to give your child a leg up in his or her schooling, build a strong foundation for future studies or address a possible learning problem, Kumon provides an effective program for developing key learning skills given the strengths and needs of each individual child.

What makes Kumon so different?

Kumon uses neither a classroom model nor a tutoring approach. It's designed to facilitate self-acquisition of the skills and study habits needed to improve academic performance. This empowers children to succeed on their own, giving them a sense of accomplishment that fosters further achievement. Whether for remedial work or enrichment, a child advances according to individual ability and initiative to reach his or her full potential. Kumon is not only effective, but also surprisingly affordable.

What is the role of the Kumon Instructor?

Kumon Instructors regard themselves more as mentors or coaches than teachers in the traditional sense. Their principal role is to provide the direction, support and encouragement that will guide the student to performing at 100% of his or her potential. Along with their rigorous training in the Kumon Method, all Kumon Instructors share a passion for education and an earnest desire to help children succeed.

KUMON FOSTERS:

- A mastery of the basics of reading and math
- Improved concentration and study habits
- Increased self-discipline and self-confidence
- A proficiency in material at every level
- Performance to each student's full potential
- A sense of accomplishment

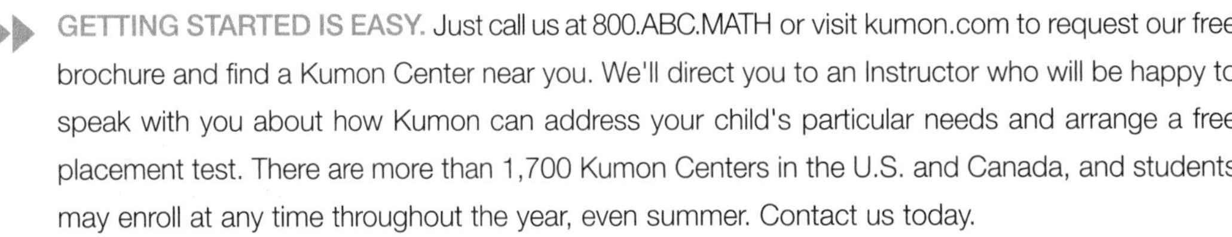
GETTING STARTED IS EASY. Just call us at 800.ABC.MATH or visit kumon.com to request our free brochure and find a Kumon Center near you. We'll direct you to an Instructor who will be happy to speak with you about how Kumon can address your child's particular needs and arrange a free placement test. There are more than 1,700 Kumon Centers in the U.S. and Canada, and students may enroll at any time throughout the year, even summer. Contact us today.

Which Is Longer?

Name

Date

■ Which is longer? Write a check (✔) next to the longer bar.

①
( )
( )

②

( )
( )

③

( )
( )

④

( )
( )

⑤
( )
( )

■ Which is longer? Write a check (✔) next to the longer bar.

① ( )
( )

② ( )
( )

③ ( )
( )

④ ( )
( )

⑤ ( )
( )

Which Is Shorter?

Name

Date

■ Which is shorter? Write a check (✔) next to the shorter bar.

① ( )
(✔)

② ( )
( )

③ ( )
( )

④ ( )
( )
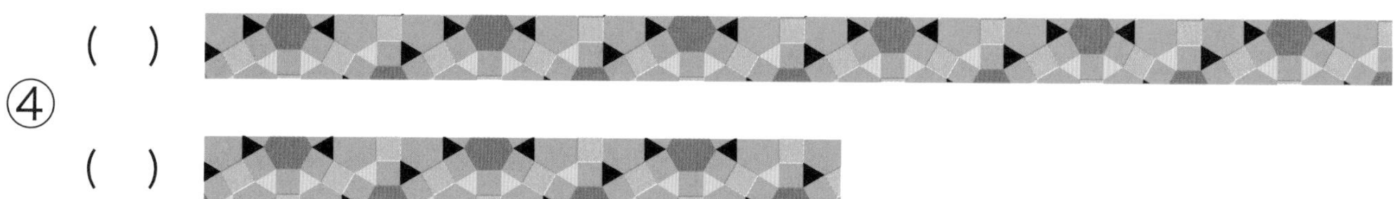

⑤ ( )
( )

■ Which is shorter? Write a check (✔) next to the shorter bar.

① ( )

( )

② ( )

( )

③ ( )

( )

④ ( )

( )

⑤ ( )

( )

Which Is the Longest?

Name
Date

■Which is the longest? Write a check (✔) next to the longest bar.

①

( ) 

( ) 

( ) 

②

( )

( )

( ) 

③

( )

( ) 

( )

( )

■Which is the longest? Write a check (✔) next to the longest bar.

( )

① ( )

( )

( )

② ( )

( )

( )

( )

③

( )

( )

Which Is the Shortest?

Name
Date

■ Which is the shortest? Write a check (✔) next to the shortest bar.

( )

① (✔)

( )

( )

② ( )

( )

( )

( )

③

( )

( )

■Which is the shortest? Write a check (✔) next to the shortest bar.

( )

① ( )

( )

( )

② ( )

( )

( )

( )

③

( )

( )

Which Is Longer?

Name

Date

■Which is longer? Write a check (✔) next to the longer object.

①
( )
( )

②
( )
( )

③
( )
( )

④
( )
( )

⑤
( )
( )

■ Which is longer? Write a check (✔) next to the longer object.

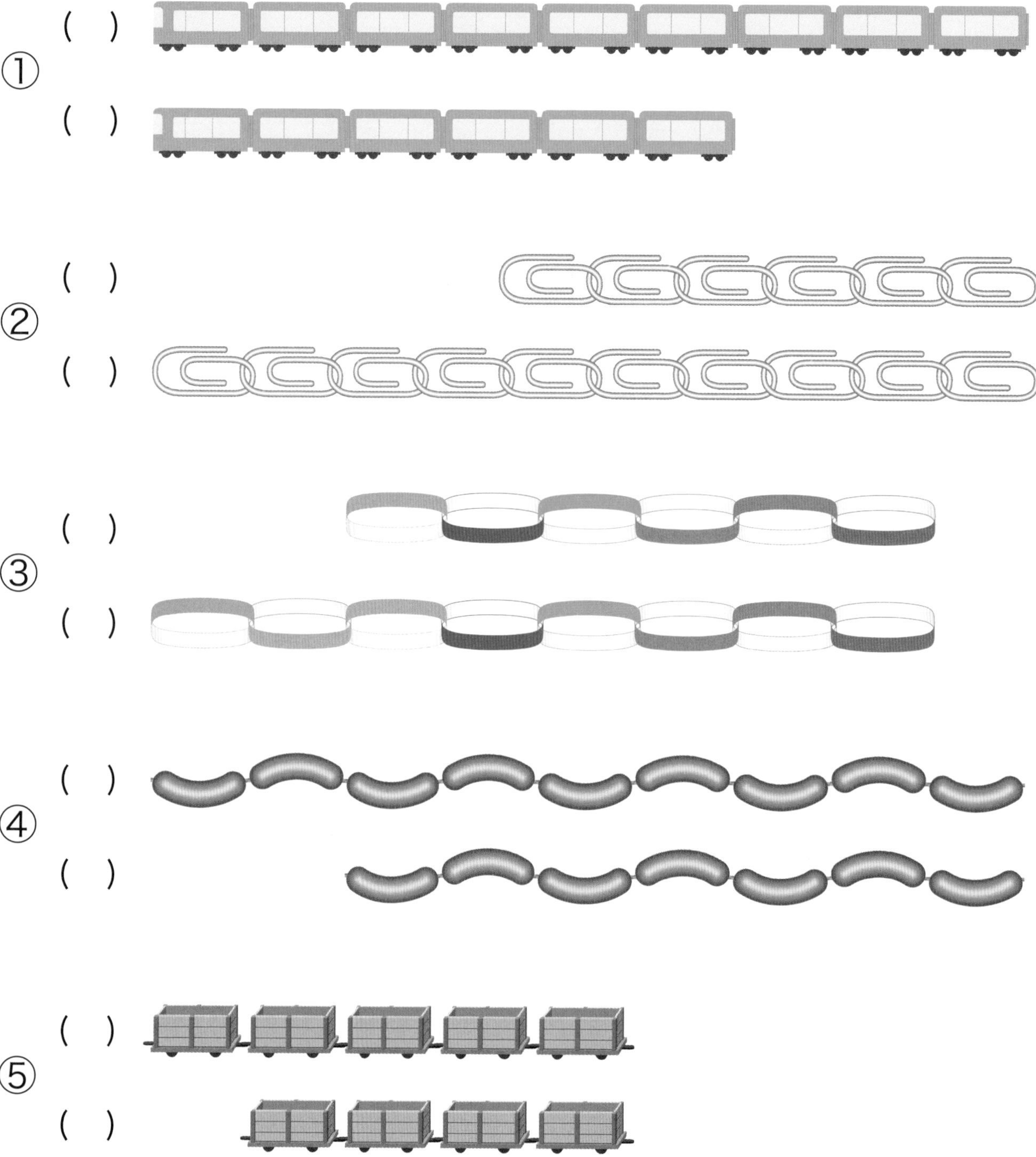

Which Is Longer?

Name
Date

To parents: If your child is having difficulty, please assist your child and say, "Let's count the number of blocks in each row together." Praise your child as he or she finishes the activity.

■ Which is longer? Write a check (✔) next to the longer row of blocks.

①
( )
( )

②
( )
( )

③
( )
( )

④
( )
( )

⑤
( )
( )

■ Which is longer? Write a check (✔) next to the longer row of blocks.

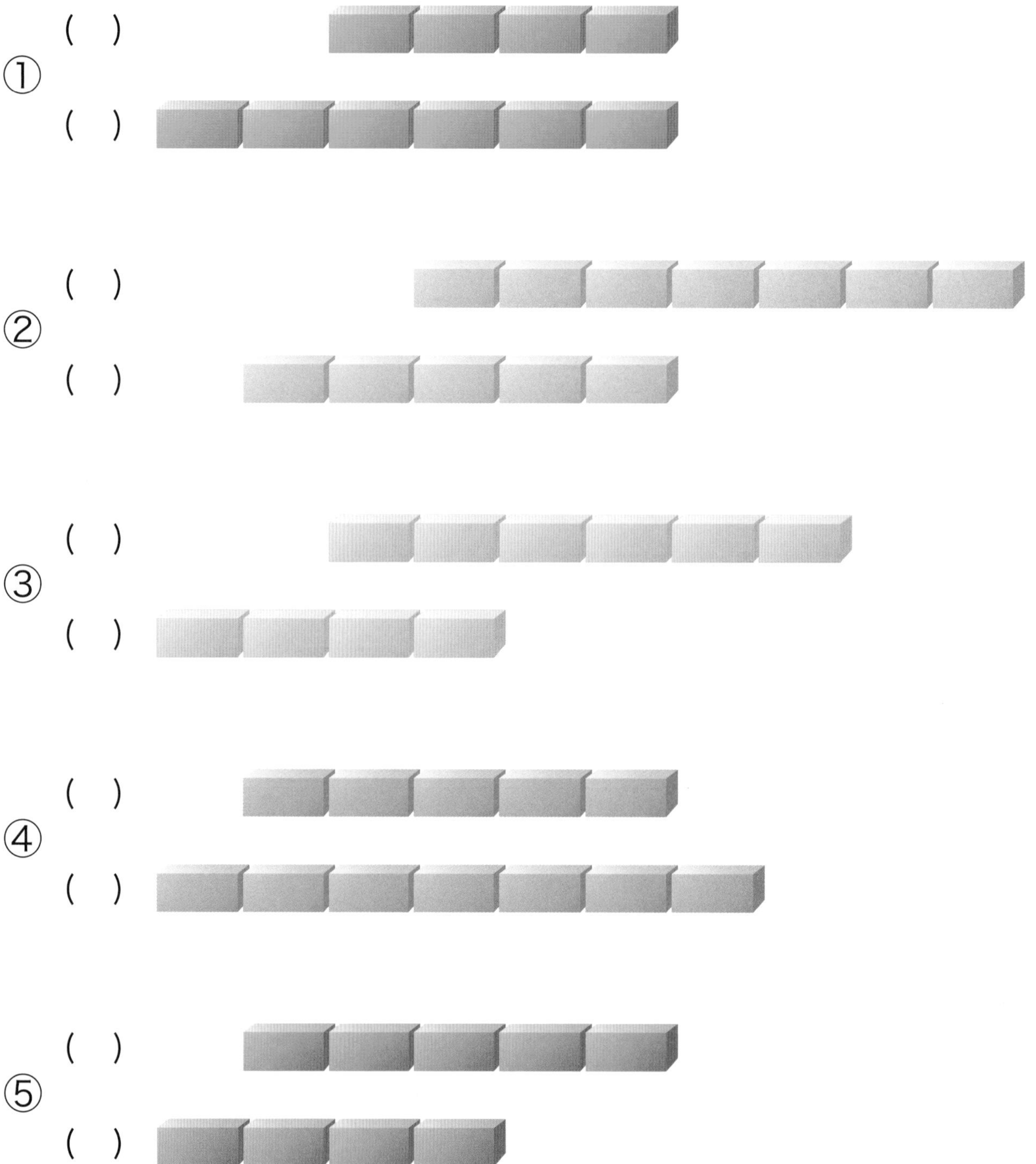

Which Is Shorter?

Name
Date

■Which is shorter? Write a check (✔) next to the shorter row of blocks.

① ( )
( )

② ( )
( )

③ ( )
( )

④ ( )
( )

⑤ ( )
( )

■ Which is shorter? Write a check (✔) next to the shorter row of blocks.

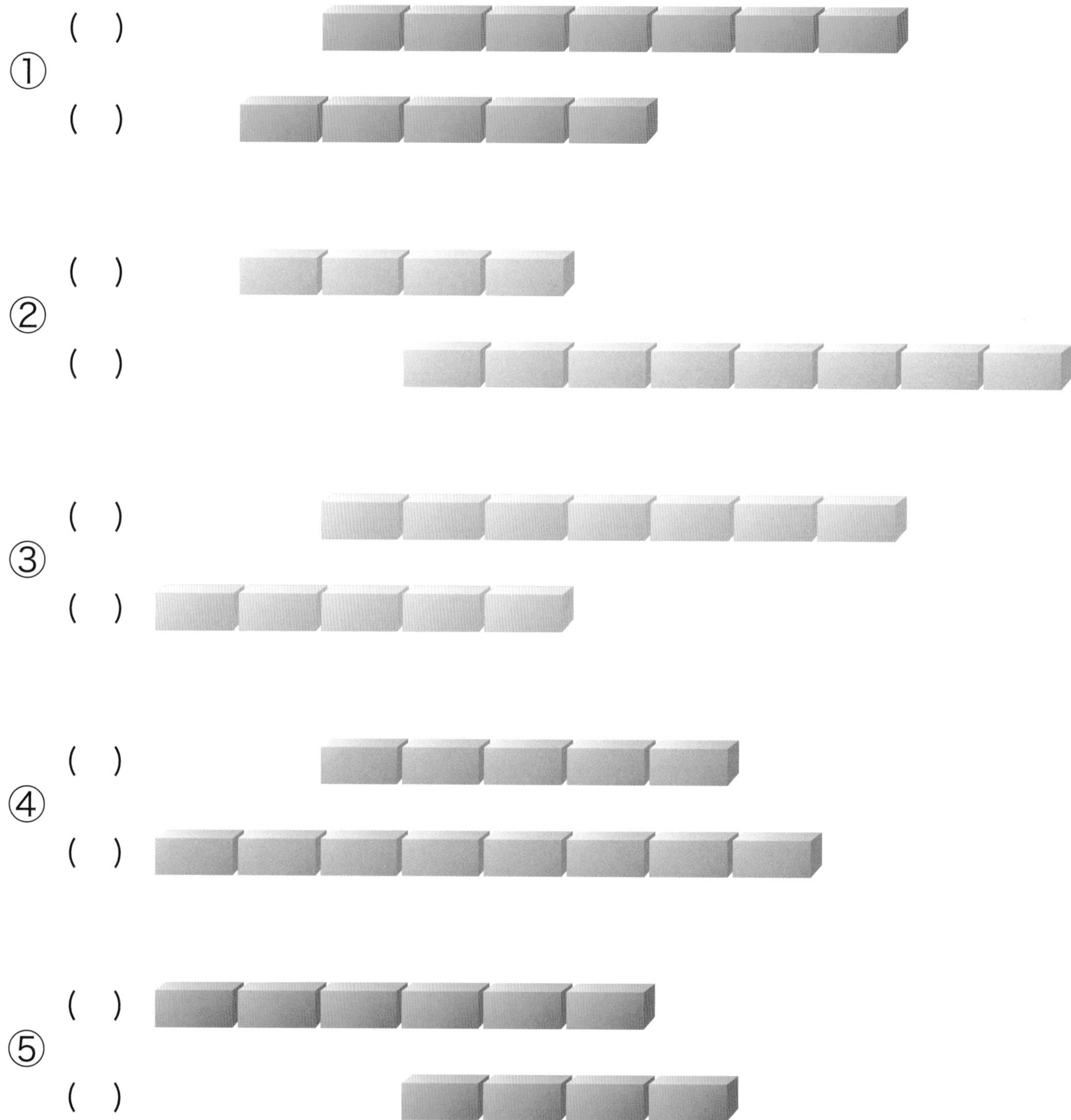

8 Longest and Shortest

Name
Date

■ Which is the longest, and which is the shortest? Write a check (✔) next to the longest row and a circle (○) next to the shortest row.

( )

① (✔)

(○)

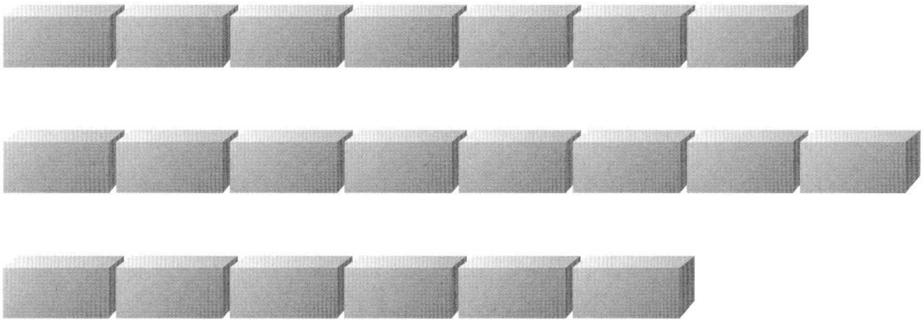

( )

② ( )

( )

( )

③ ( )

( )

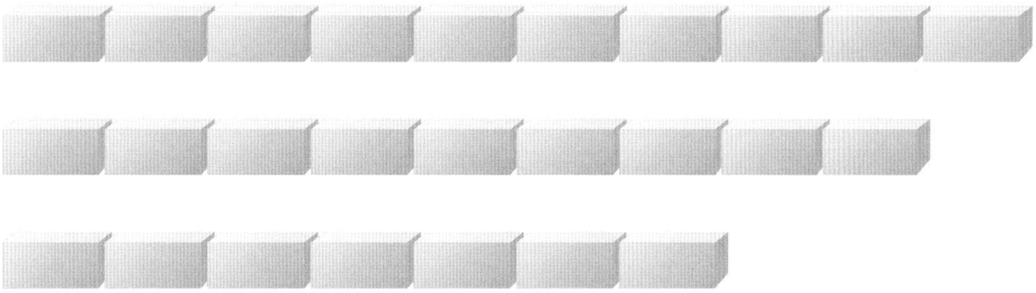

( )

④ ( )

( )

■ Which is the longest, and which is the shortest? Write a check (✔) next to the longest row and a circle (○) next to the shortest row.

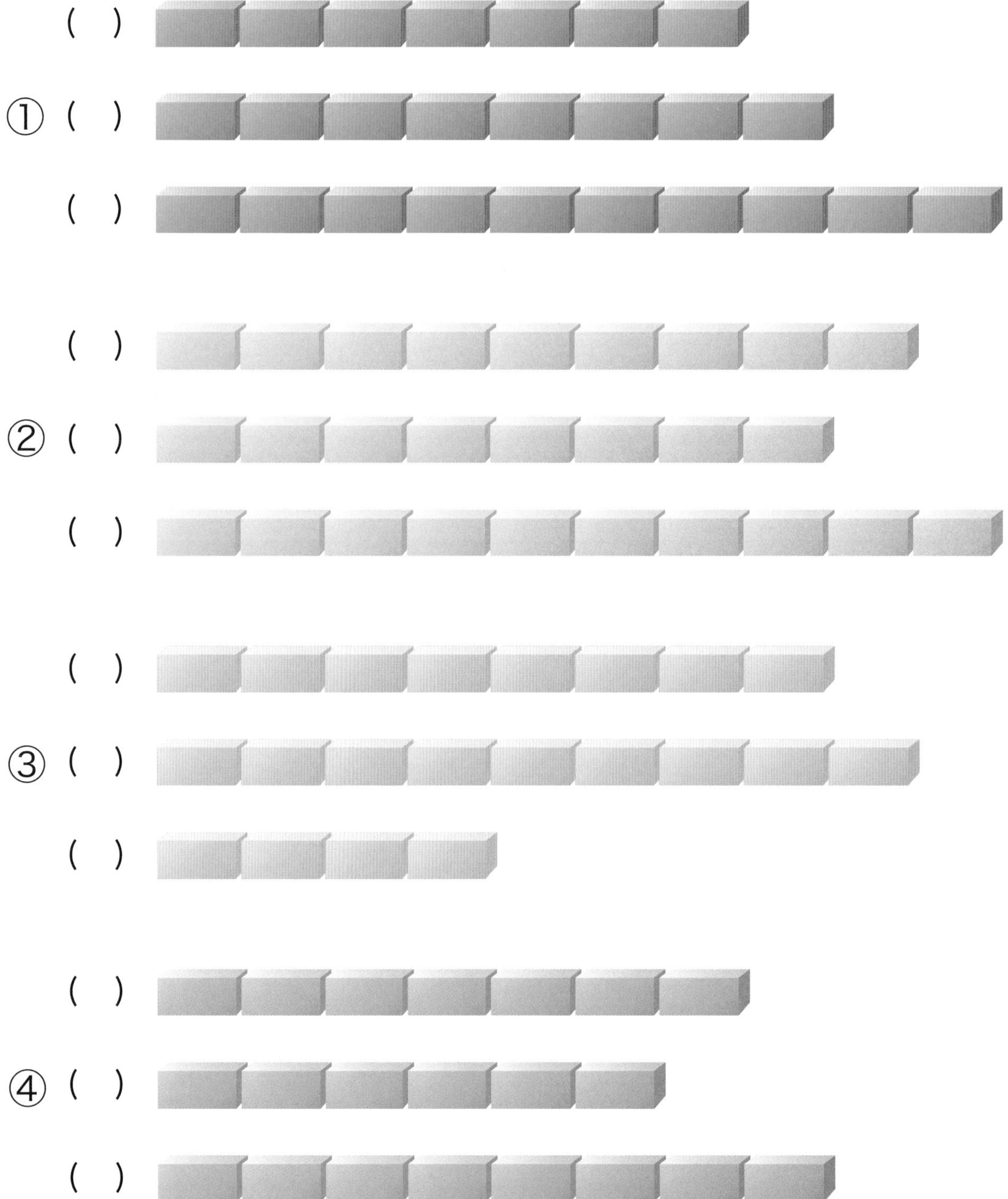

Longest and Shortest

Name
Date

■ Which is the longest, and which is the shortest? Write a check (✔) next to the longest row and a circle (◯) next to the shortest row.

( )

① ( )

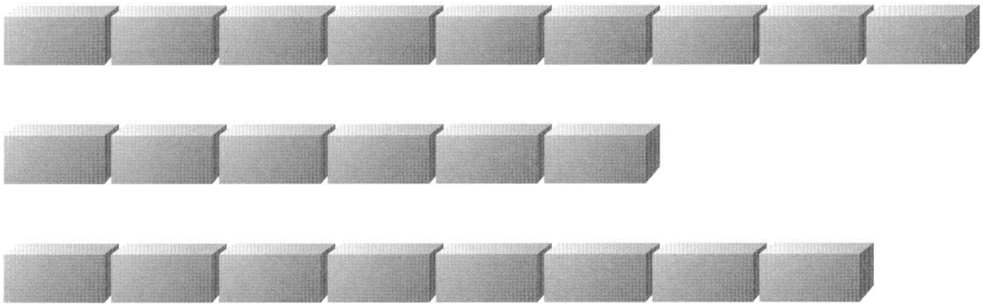

( )

( )

② ( )

( )

( )

③ ( )

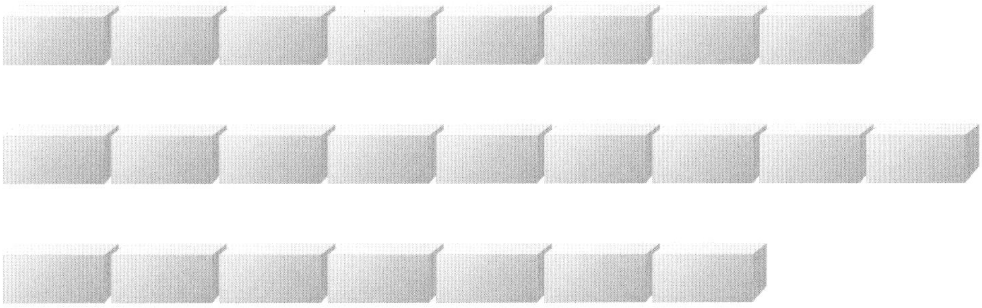

( )

( )

④ ( )

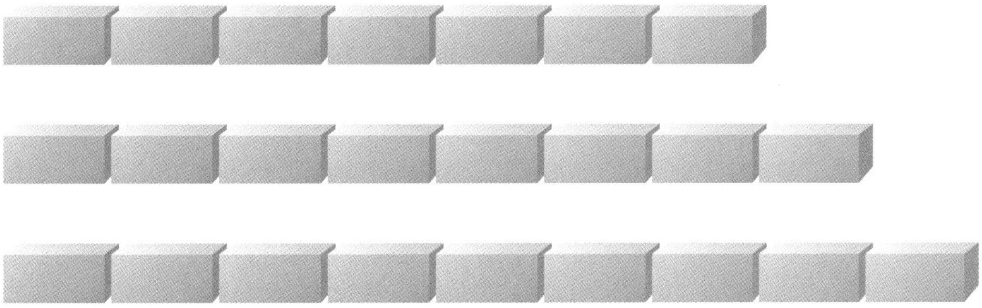

( )

■ Which is the longest, and which is the shortest? Write a check (✔) next to the longest row and a circle (○) next to the shortest row.

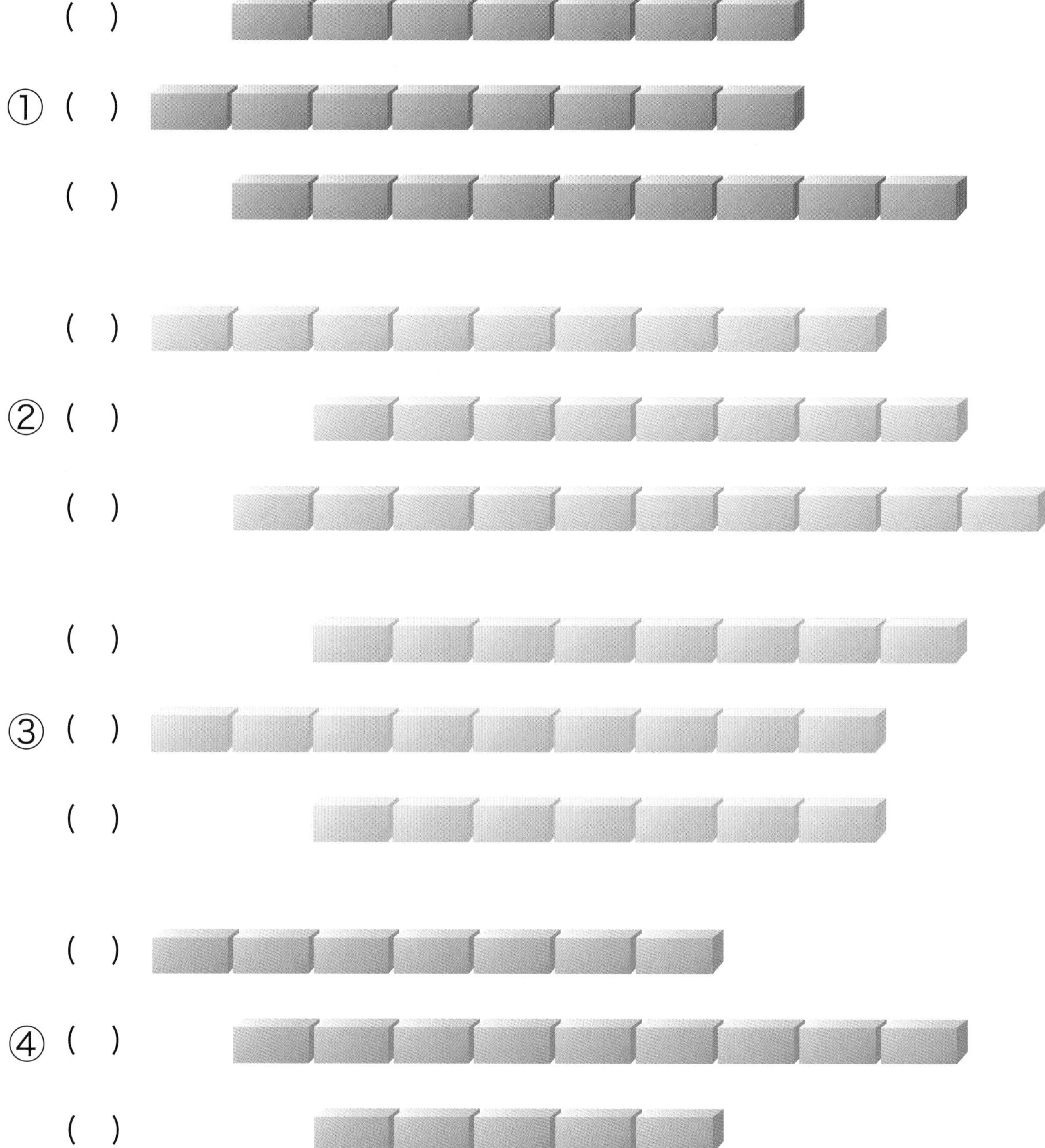

Longest and Shortest

Name

Date

■ Which is the longest, and which is the shortest? Write a check (✔) next to the longest row and a circle (◯) next to the shortest row.

①

( )

( )

( )

( )

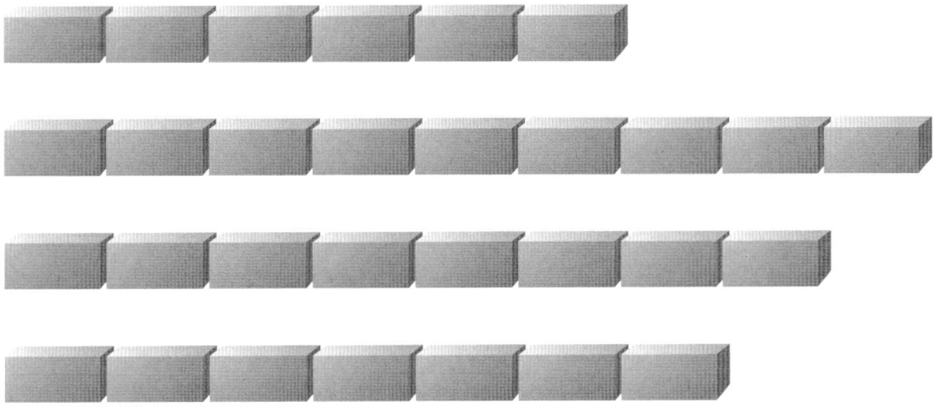

②

( )

( )

( )

( )

③

( )

( )

( )

( )

■ Which is the longest, and which is the shortest? Write a check (✔) next to the longest row and a circle (◯) next to the shortest row.

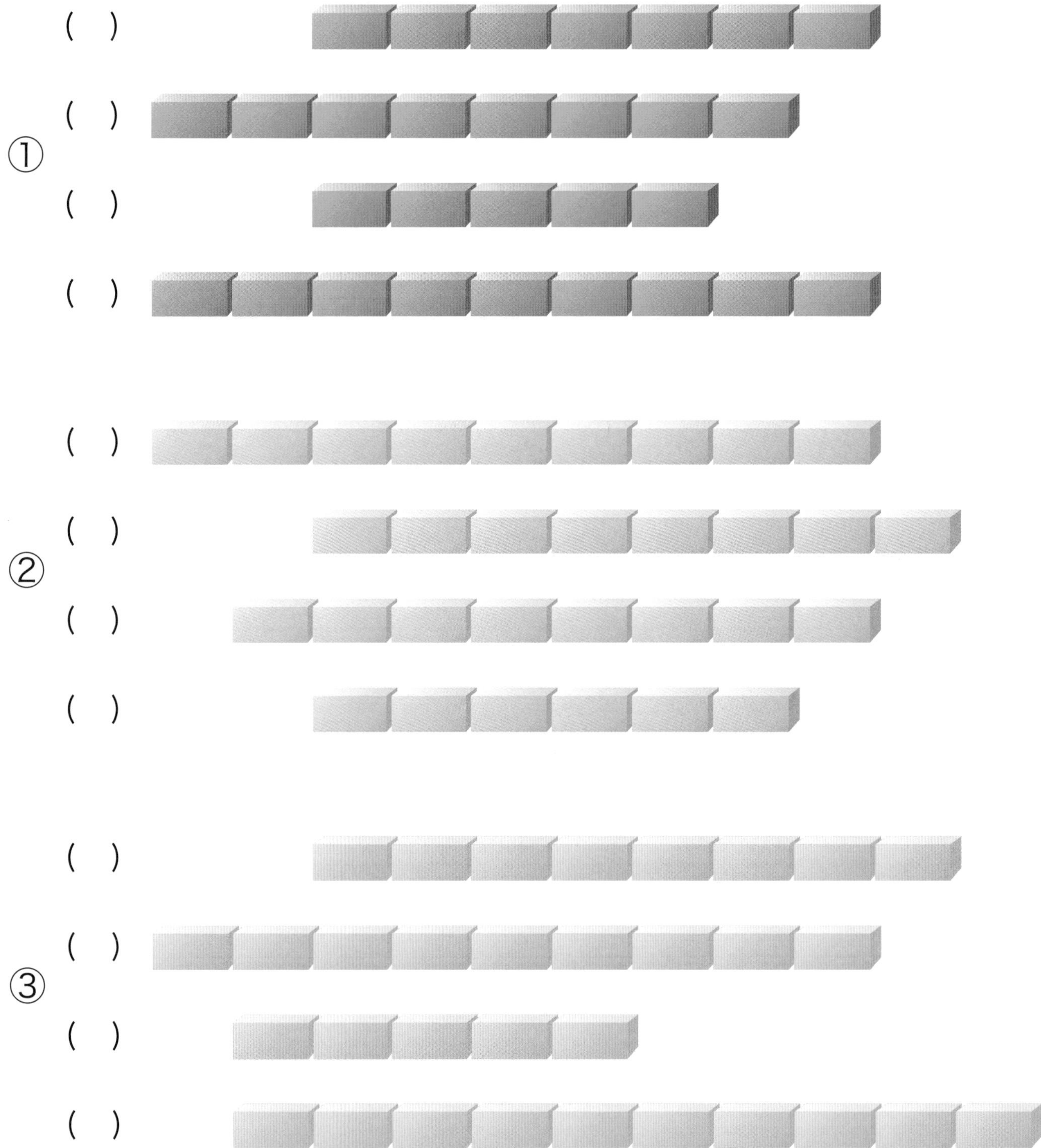

Longest and Shortest

Name

Date

■Which is the longest, and which is the shortest? Write a check (✔) next to the longest line and a circle (◯) next to the shortest line.

( )

① ( )

( )

( )

② ( )

( )

( )

③ ( )

( )

( )

④ ( )

( )

■ Which is the longest, and which is the shortest? Write a check (✔) next to the longest line and a circle (○) next to the shortest line.

( )

① ( )

( )

( )

② ( )

( )

( )

③ ( )

( )

( )

④ ( )

( )

Longest and Shortest

Name
Date

■ Which is the longest, and which is the shortest? Write a check (✔) next to the longest line and a circle (○) next to the shortest line.

( ) 

① ( ) 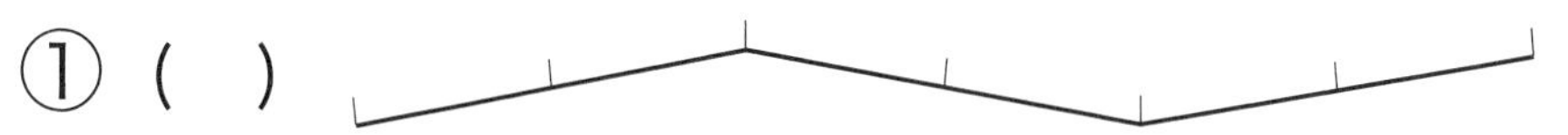

( ) 

( )

② ( )

( )

( )

③ ( )

( )

( )

④ ( )

( )

■Which is the longest, and which is the shortest? Write a check (✔) next to the longest line and a circle (○) next to the shortest line.

( )

① ( )

( )

( )

② ( )

( )

( )

③ ( )

( )

( )

④ ( )

( )

13 Equal Lengths

Name

Date

■ Color the top row of blocks to match the length of the bottom row.

①

②

③

④

⑤

To parents: If your child is having difficulty, please assist your child and advise, "First count the number of colored blocks in the bottom row. Then color the same amount of blocks in the top row starting on the left." Praise your child as he or she finishes the activity.

■Color the top row of blocks to match the length of the bottom row.

①

②

③

④

⑤

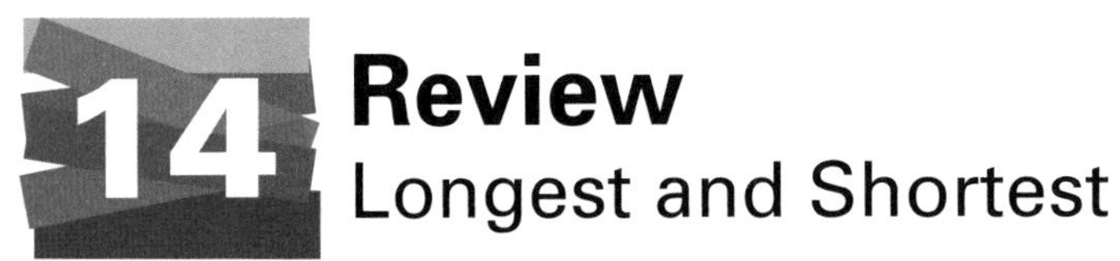

14 Review
Longest and Shortest

Name

Date

■ Which is the longest, and which is the shortest? Write a check (✔) next to the longest row and a circle (○) next to the shortest row.

①
( )
( )
( )

②
( )
( )
( )

③
( )
( )
( )

④
( )
( )
( )
( )

■ Which is the longest, and which is the shortest? Write a check (✔) next to the longest line and a circle (○) next to the shortest line.

①
( )
( )
( )

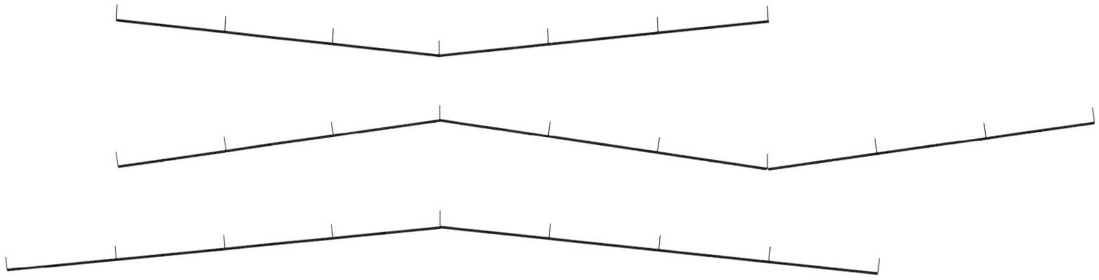

②
( )
( )
( )

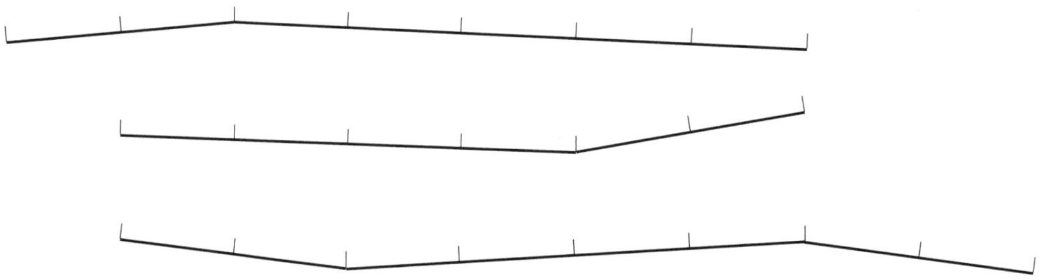

③
( )
( )
( )

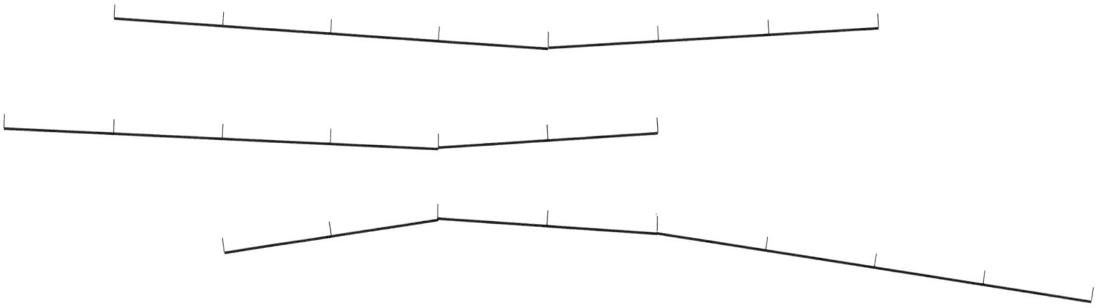

④
( )
( )
( )
( )

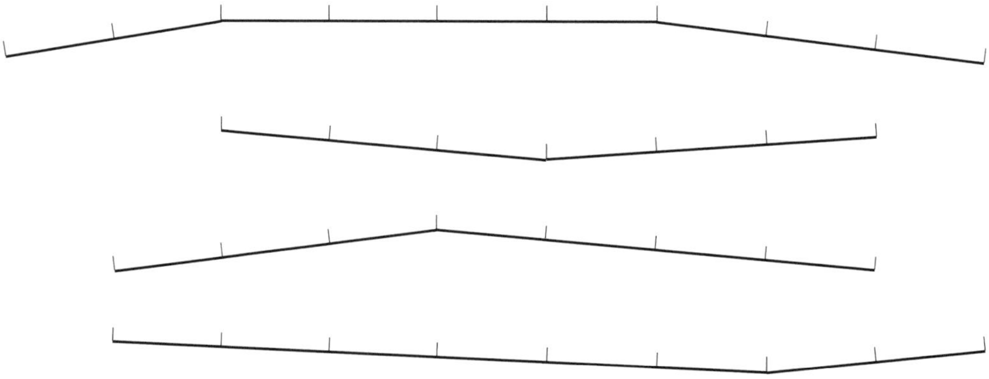

15 Practicing Numbers 1 to 100

Name

Date

■ Trace each number while saying it aloud.

1	2	3	4	5	6	7	8	9	10
11	12	13	14	15	16	17	18	19	20
21	22	23	24	25	26	27	28	29	30
31	32	33	34	35	36	37	38	39	40
41	42	43	44	45	46	47	48	49	50
51	52	53	54	55	56	57	58	59	60
61	62	63	64	65	66	67	68	69	70
71	72	73	74	75	76	77	78	79	80
81	82	83	84	85	86	87	88	89	90
91	92	93	94	95	96	97	98	99	100

■ Trace each number while saying it aloud.

1	2	3	4	5	6	7	8	9	10
11	12	13	14	15	16	17	18	19	20
21	22	23	24	25	26	27	28	29	30
31	32	33	34	35	36	37	38	39	40
41	42	43	44	45	46	47	48	49	50
51	52	53	54	55	56	57	58	59	60
61	62	63	64	65	66	67	68	69	70
71	72	73	74	75	76	77	78	79	80
81	82	83	84	85	86	87	88	89	90
91	92	93	94	95	96	97	98	99	100

16 Practicing Numbers 1 to 100

Name
Date

■ Trace each number while saying it aloud.

1	2	3	4	5	6	7	8	9	10
11	12	13	14	15	16	17	18	19	20
21	22	23	24	25	26	27	28	29	30
31	32	33	34	35	36	37	38	39	40
41	42	43	44	45	46	47	48	49	50
51	52	53	54	55	56	57	58	59	60
61	62	63	64	65	66	67	68	69	70
71	72	73	74	75	76	77	78	79	80
81	82	83	84	85	86	87	88	89	90
91	92	93	94	95	96	97	98	99	100

■Write each number while saying it aloud.

1	2	3	4	5	6	7	8	9	10
11	12	13	14	15	16	17	18	19	20
21	22	23	24	25	26	27	28	29	30
31	32	33	34	35	36	37	38	39	40
41	42	43	44	45	46	47	48	49	50
51	52	53	54	55	56	57	58	59	60
61	62	63	64	65	66	67	68	69	70
71	72	73	74	75	76	77	78	79	80
81	82	83	84	85	86	87	88	89	90
91	92	93	94	95	96	97	98	99	100

17 Practicing Numbers 1 to 100

Name
Date

■Write the missing number in each box.

1		3		5		7			10
	12	13			16		18		
21			24		26			29	30
31		33		35			38	39	
		43			46	47		49	
	52		54		56				60
61		63			66	67	68	69	
71			74			77			80
	82	83		85			88		
91		93			96	97			100

■Write the missing number in each box.

1	2		4		6		8	9	10
11			14	15		17		19	20
	22	23		25		27	28		
	32		34		36	37			40
41	42		44	45			48		50
51		53		55		57	58	59	
	62		64	65					70
	72	73		75	76		78	79	
81			84		86	87		89	90
	92		94	95			98	99	100

Inches

Name
Date

Read the ruler from left to right. Fill in the missing number.

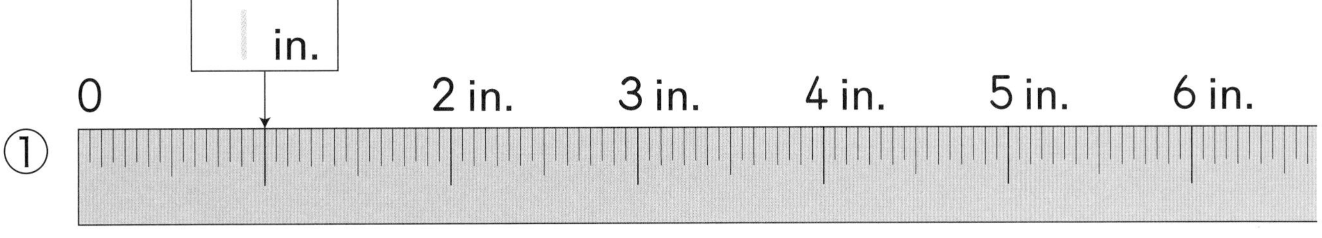

①

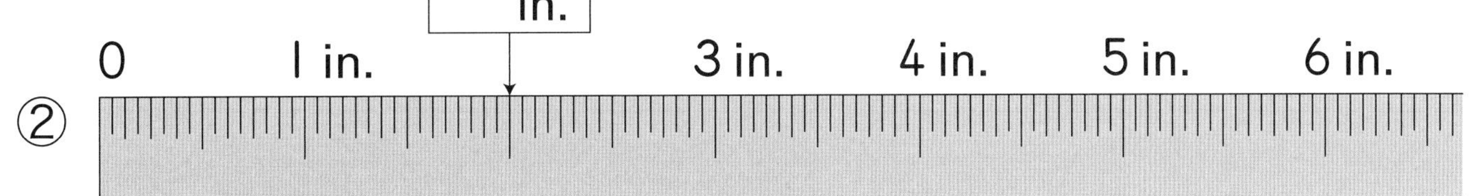

②

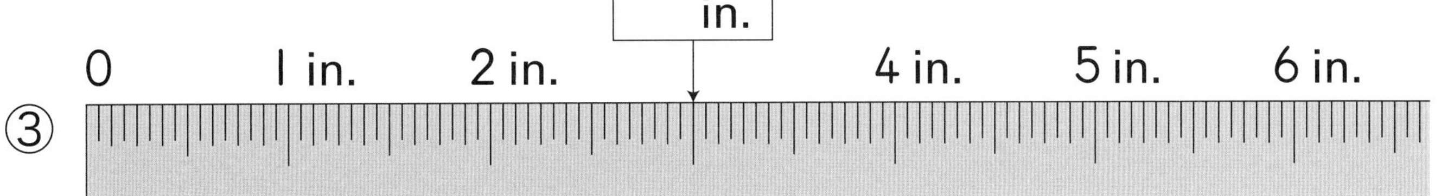

③

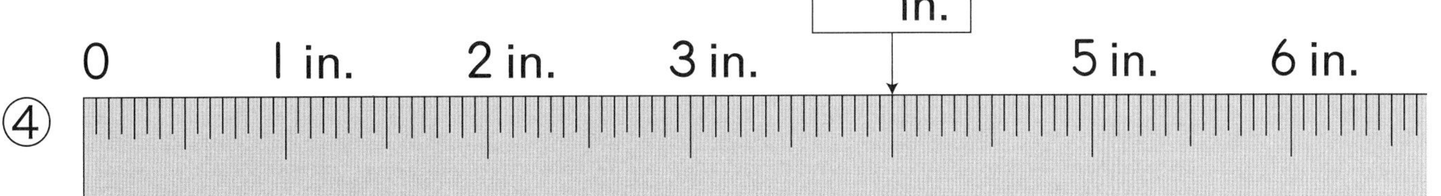

④

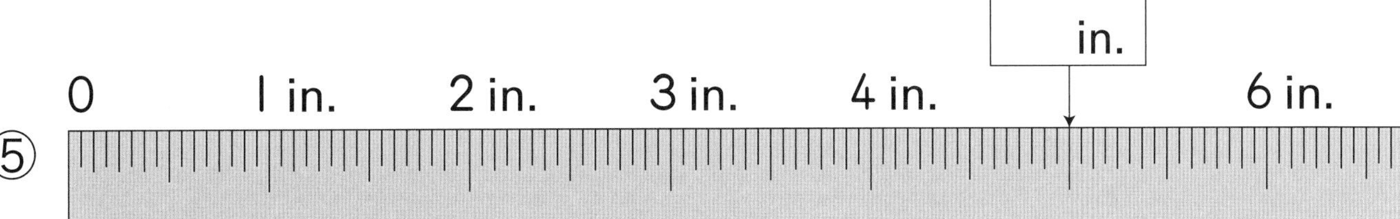

⑤

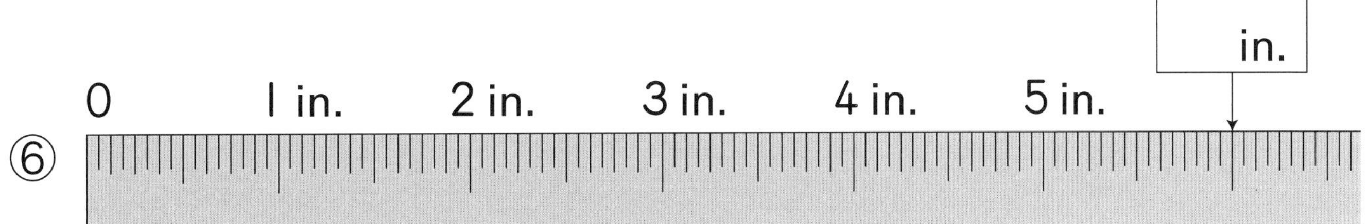

⑥

■ Read the ruler from left to right. Fill in the missing number.

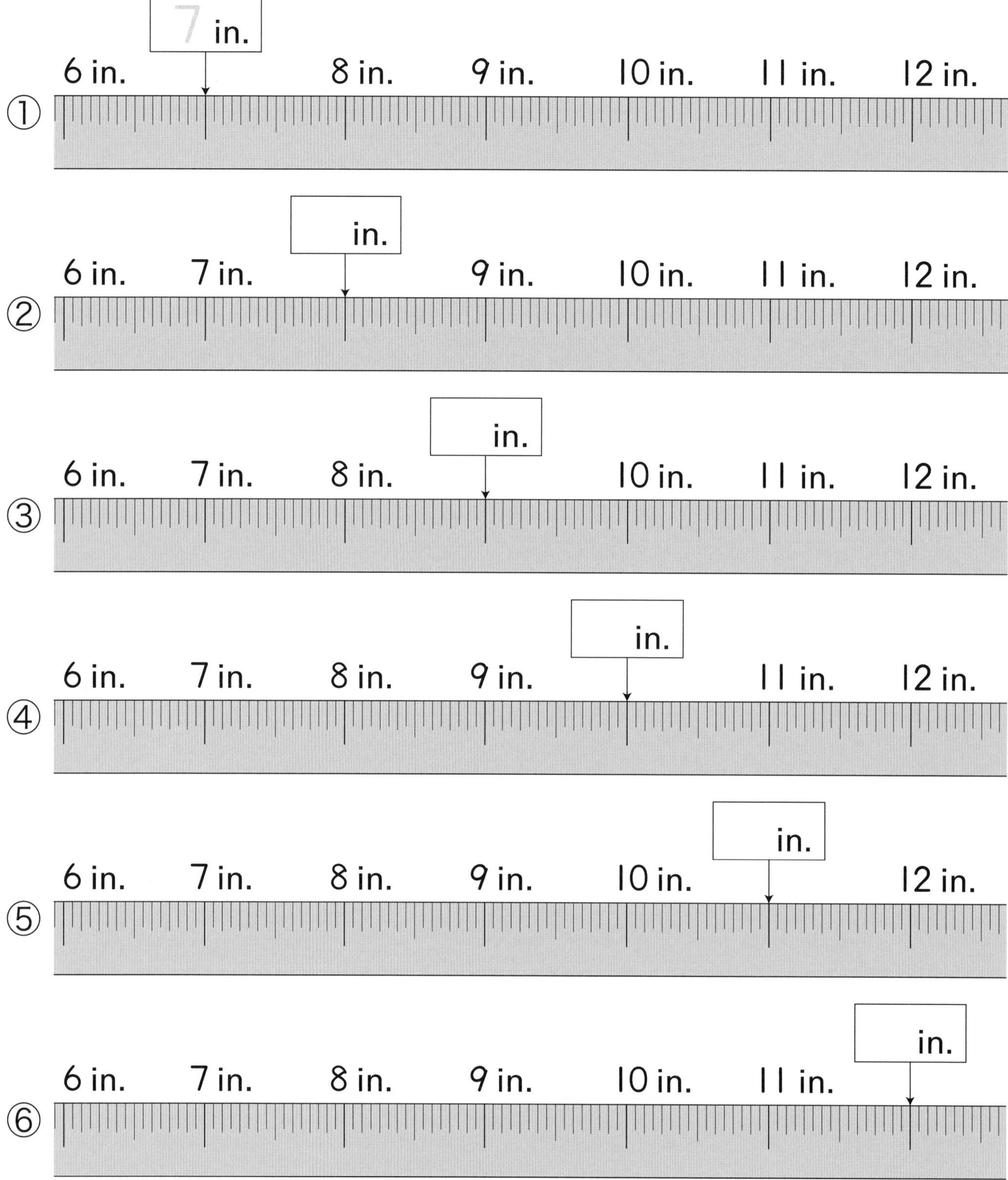

19 Inches

Name	
Date	

■ Read the ruler from left to right. Fill in the missing numbers.

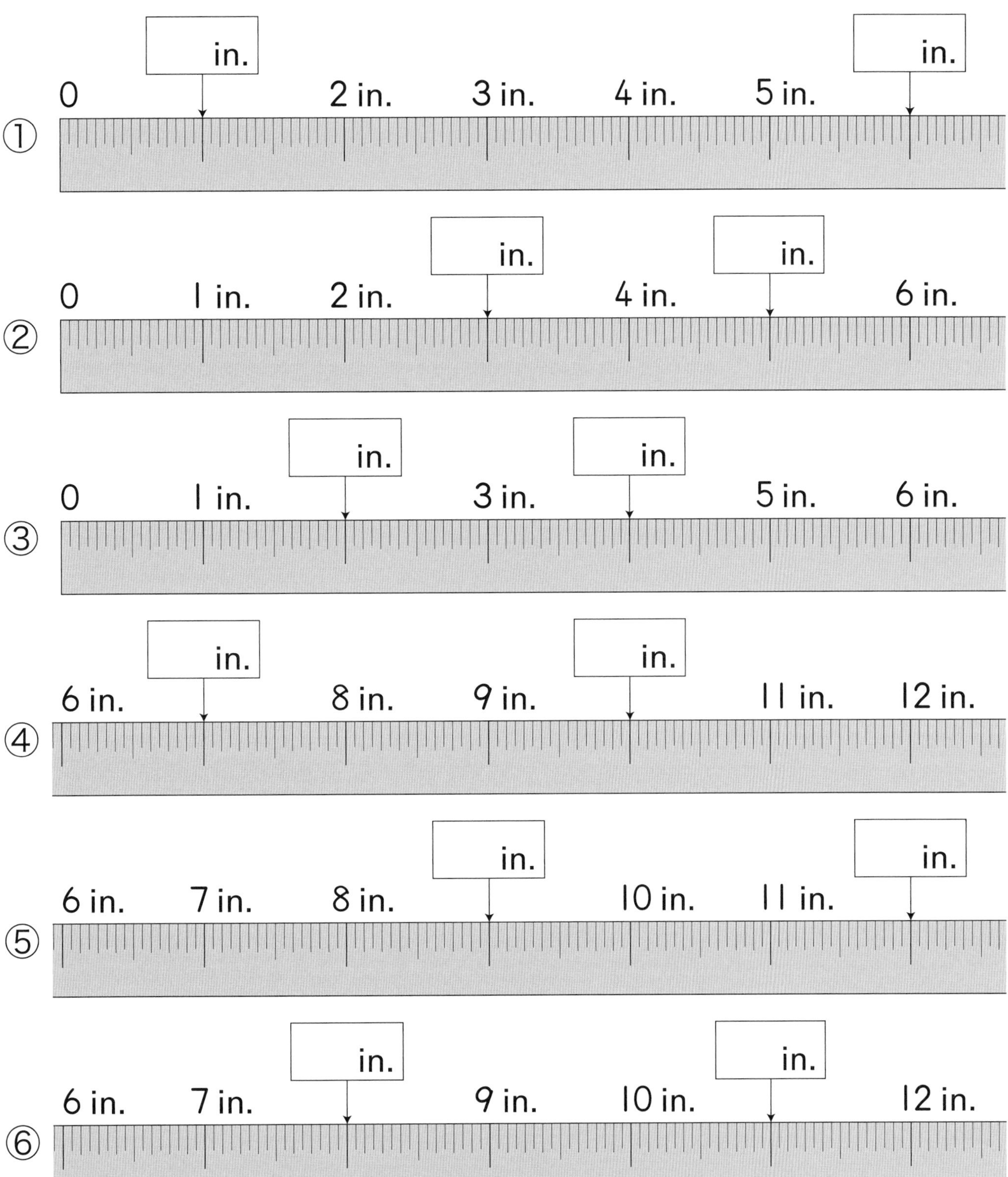

■ Read the ruler from left to right. Fill in the missing numbers.

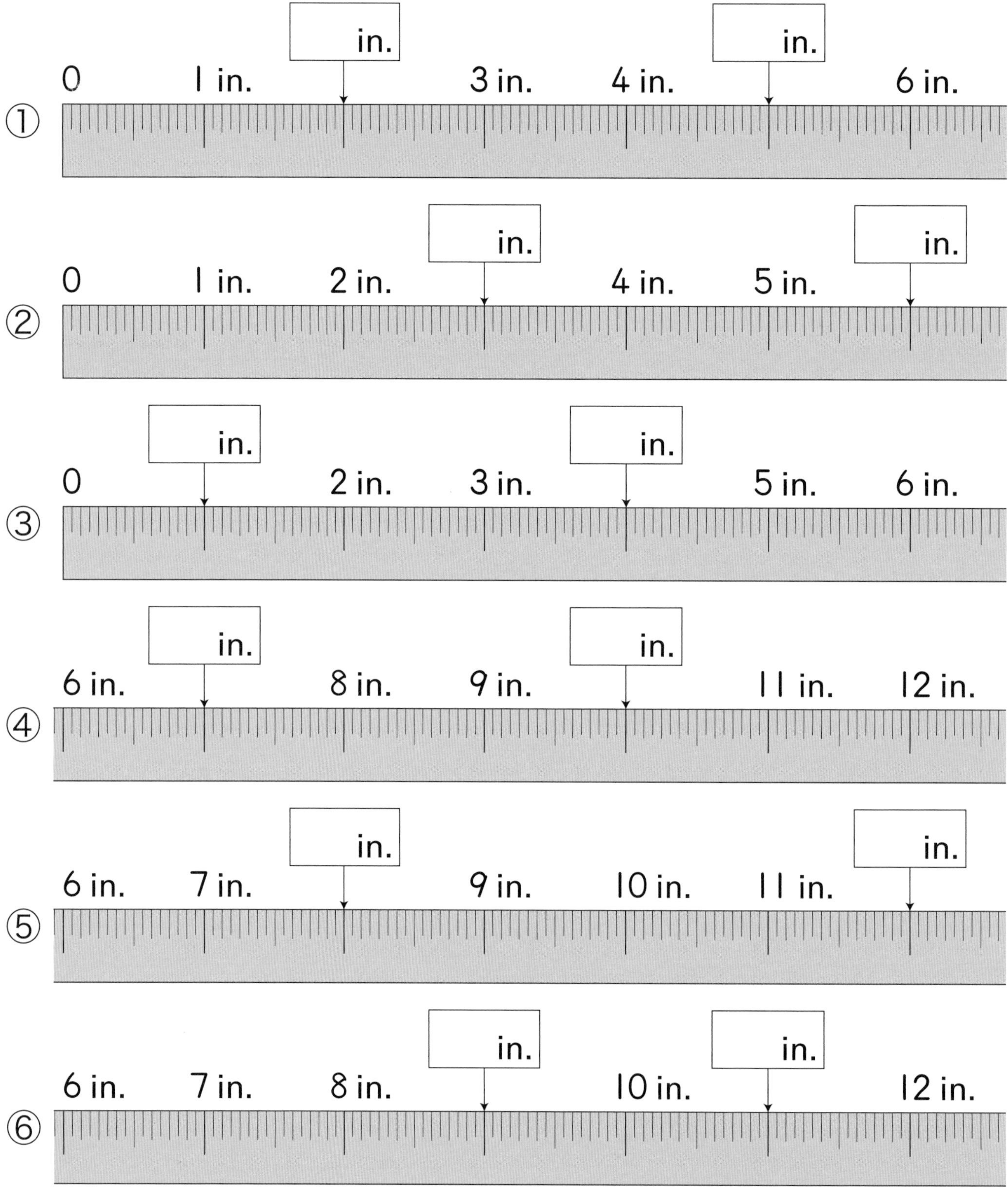

Inches

Name

Date

Read the ruler from left to right. Fill in the missing number.

① 0 [ ] in.

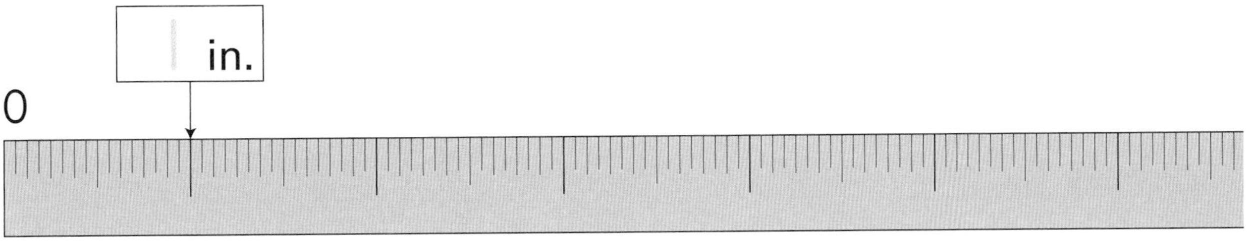

② 0 [ ] in.

③ 0 [ ] in.

④ 0 [ ] in.

⑤ 0 [ ] in.

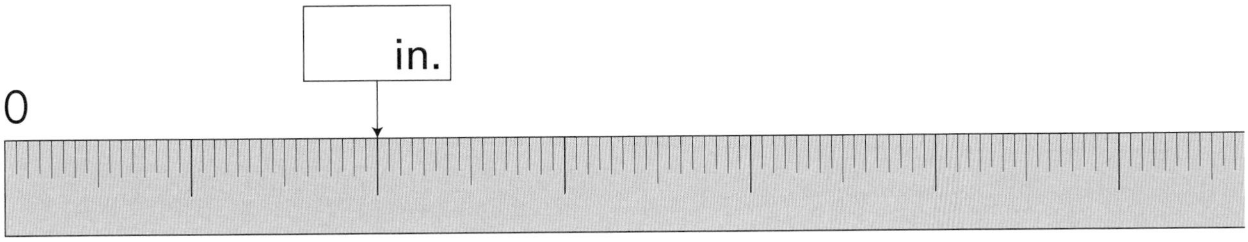

⑥ 0 [ ] in.

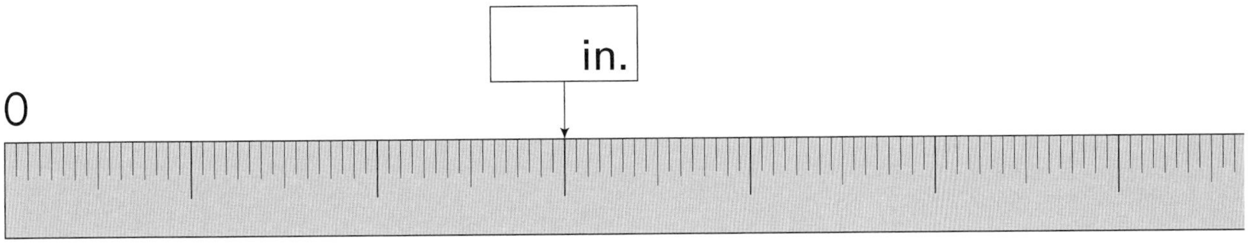

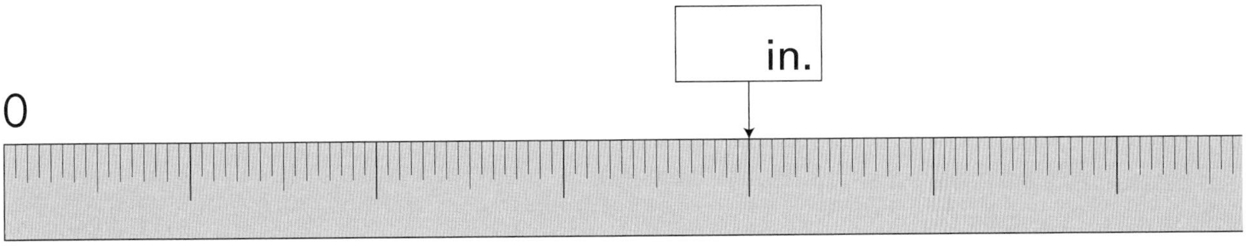

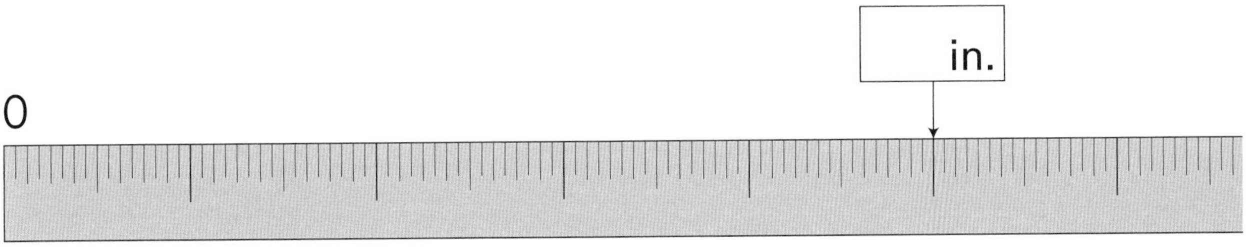

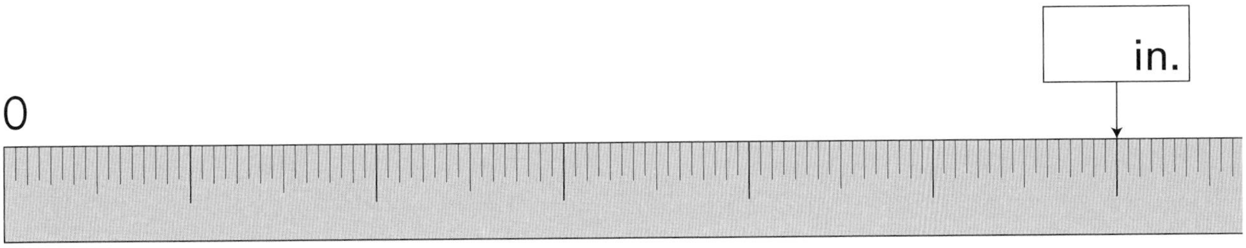

■Read the ruler from left to right. Fill in the missing number.

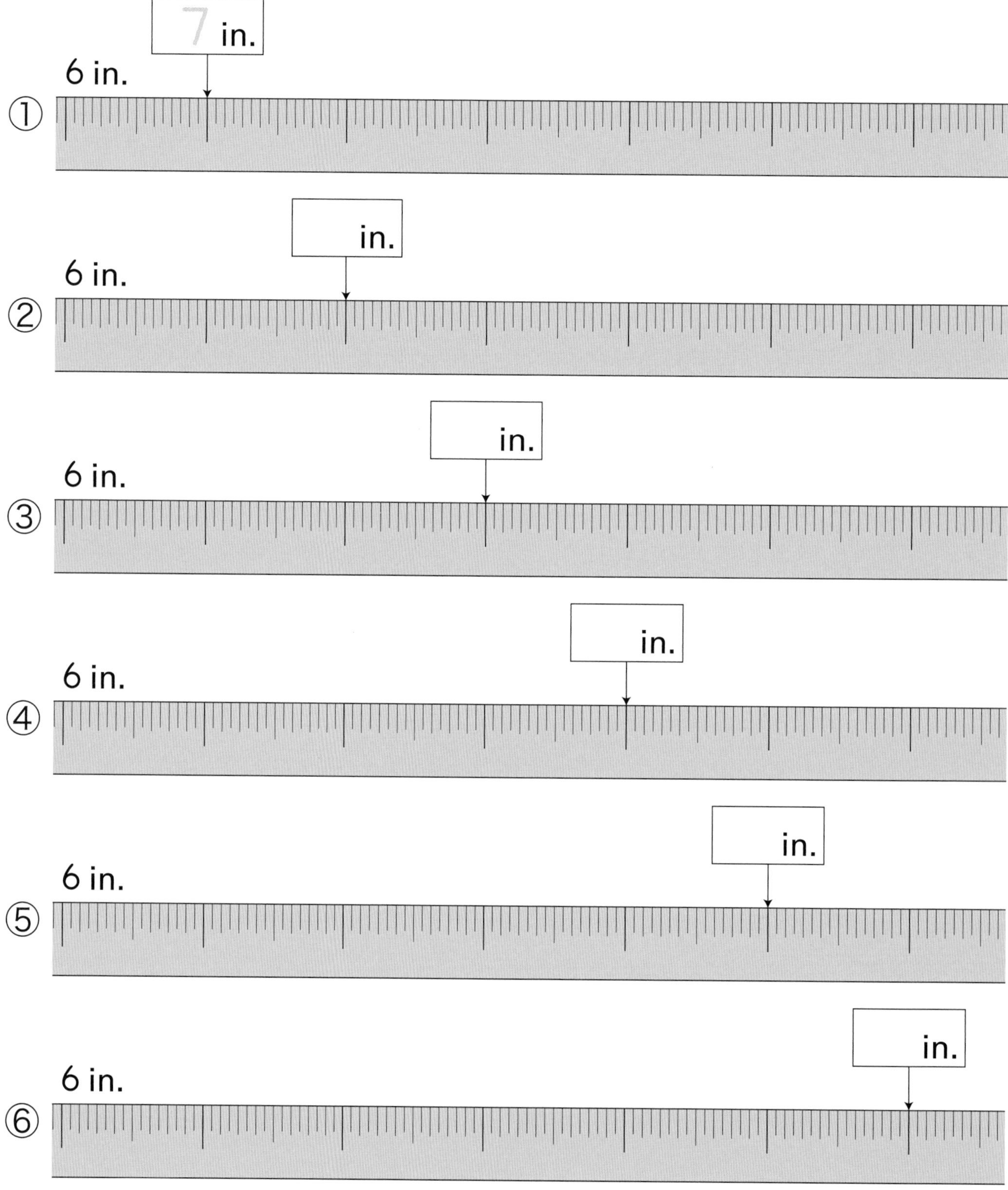

Inches

Name

Date

Read the ruler from left to right. Fill in the missing numbers.

① 0 — in. — in.

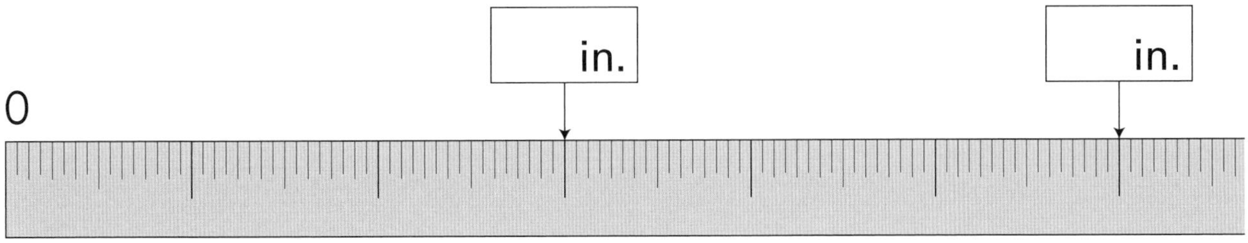

② 0 — in. — in.

③ 0 — in. — in.

④ 6 in. — in. — in.

⑤ 6 in. — in. — in.

⑥ 6 in. — in. — in.

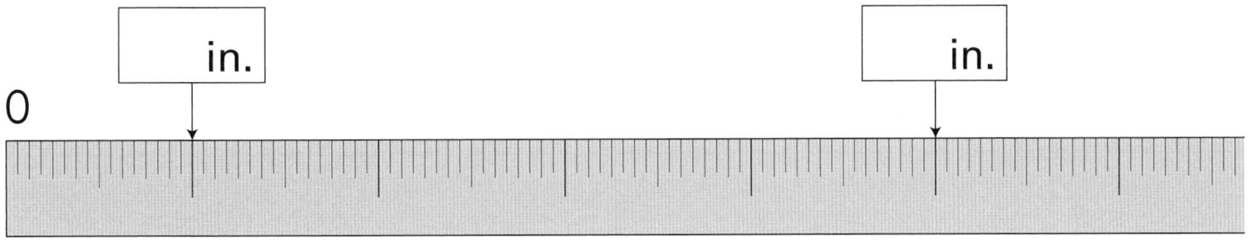

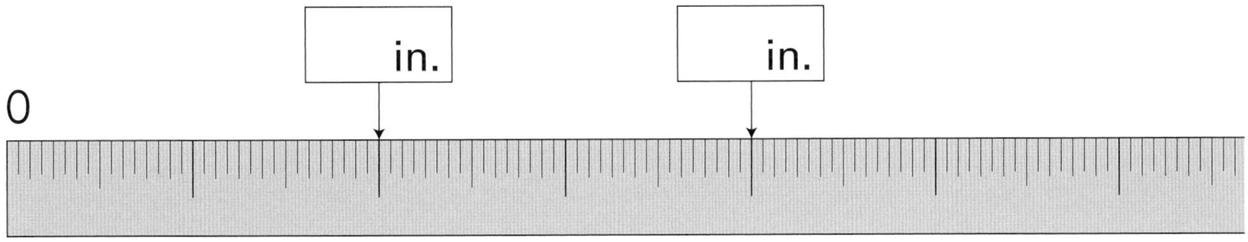

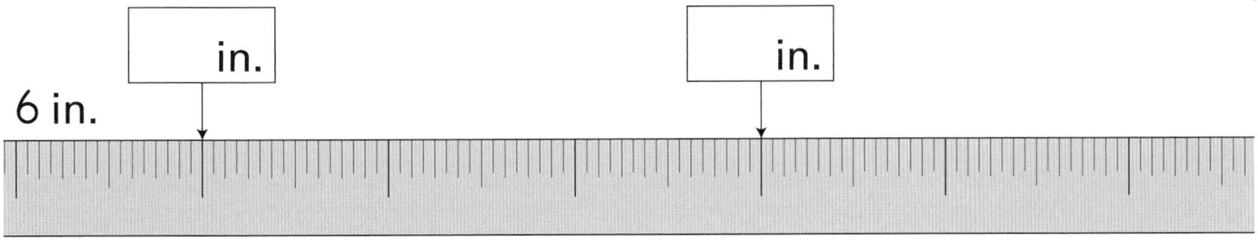

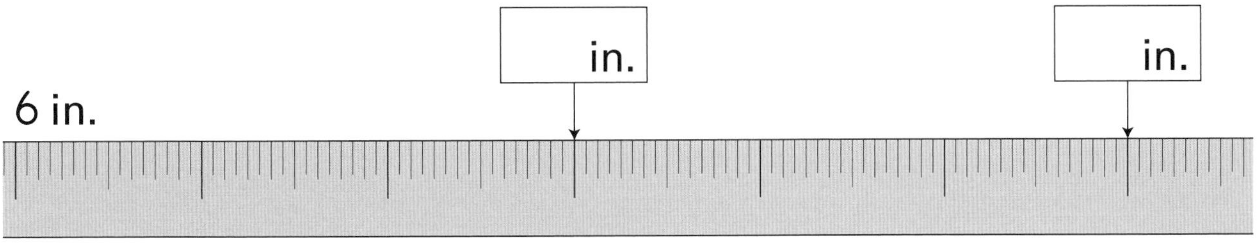

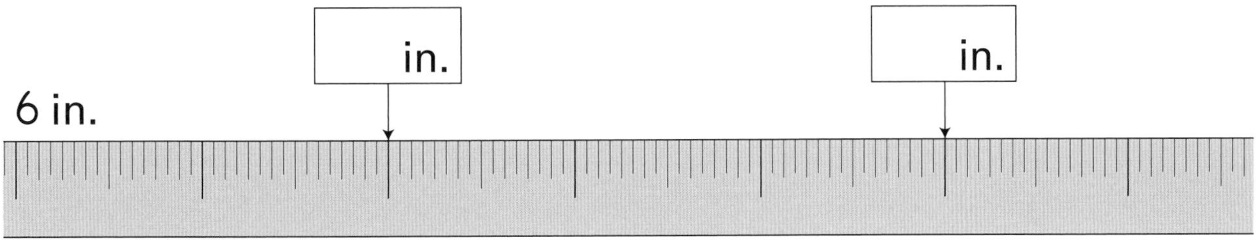

■Read the ruler from left to right. Fill in the missing numbers.

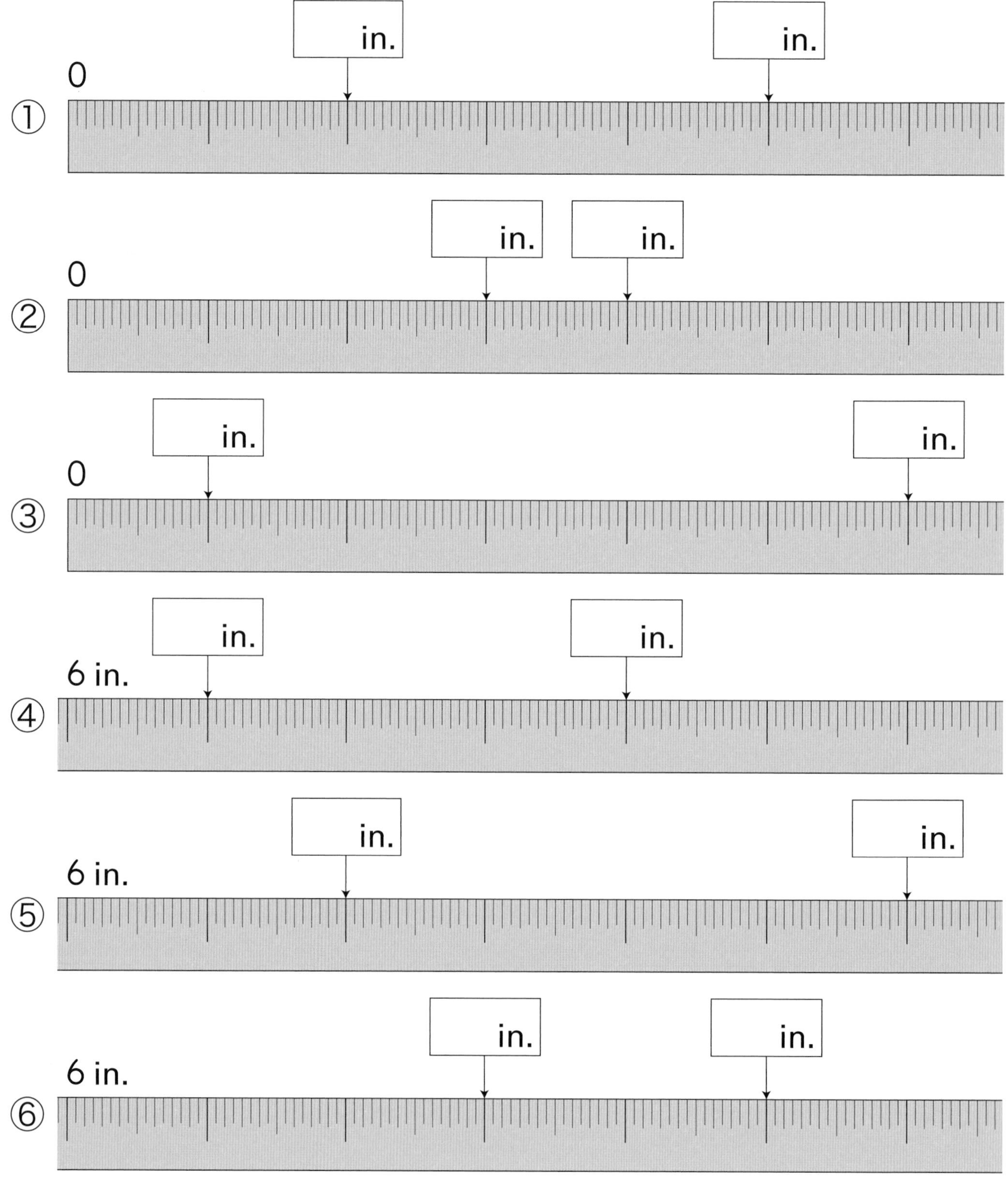

Measuring in Inches

Name
Date

■ How long is each yellow line? Answer in inches.

①

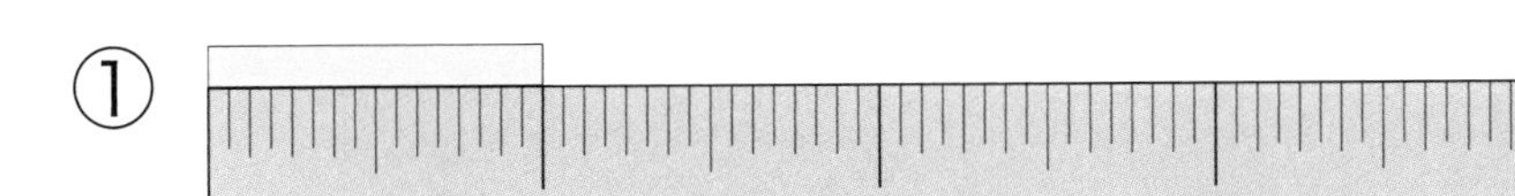

________ in.

②

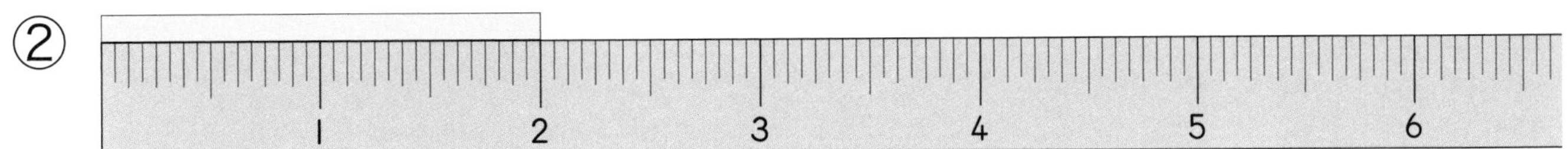

________ in.

③

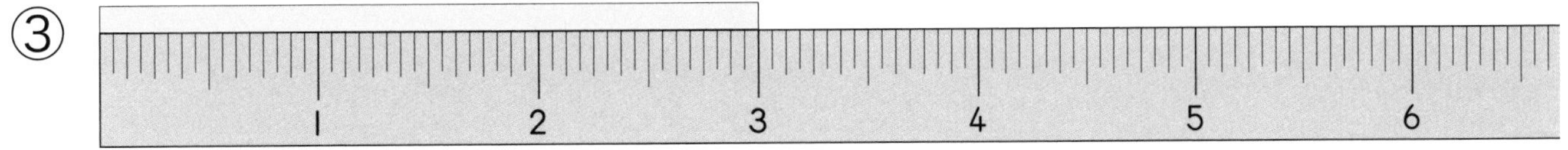

________ in.

④

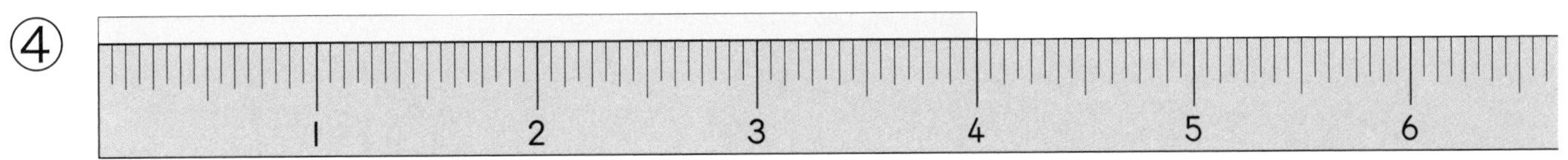

________ in.

⑤

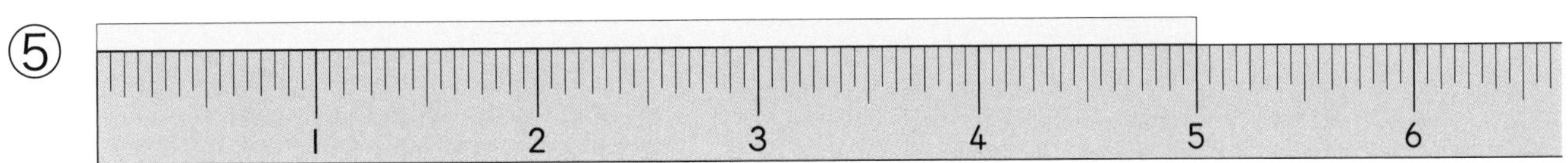

________ in.

■ How long is each yellow line? Answer in inches.

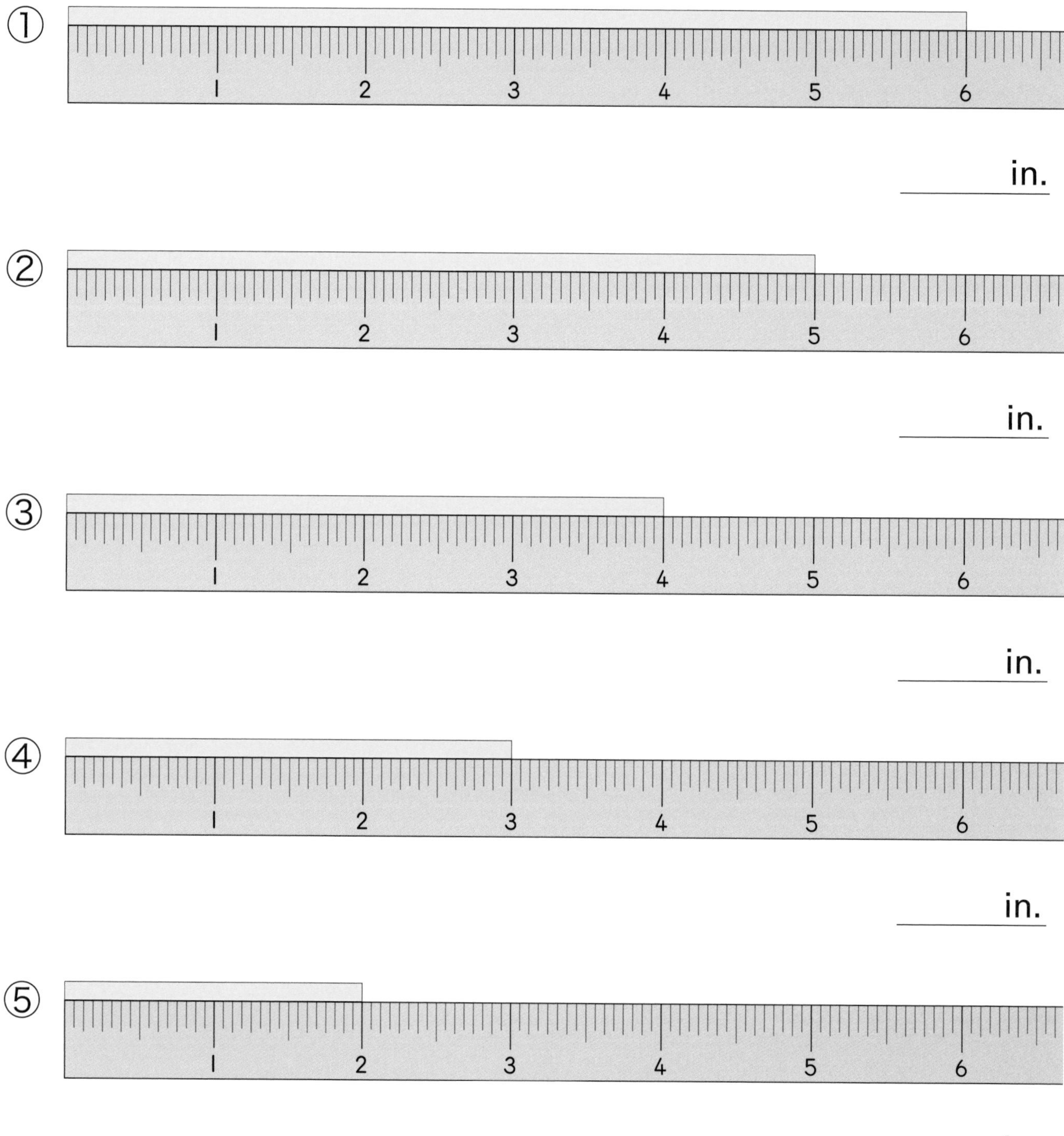

23 Measuring in Inches

Name

Date

■ How long is each yellow line? Answer in inches.

① 

______ in.

② 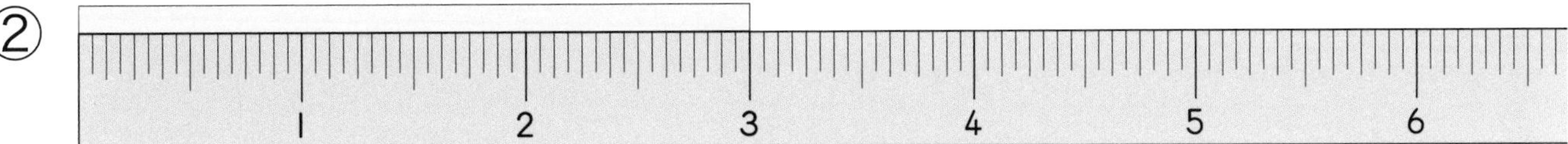

______ in.

③ 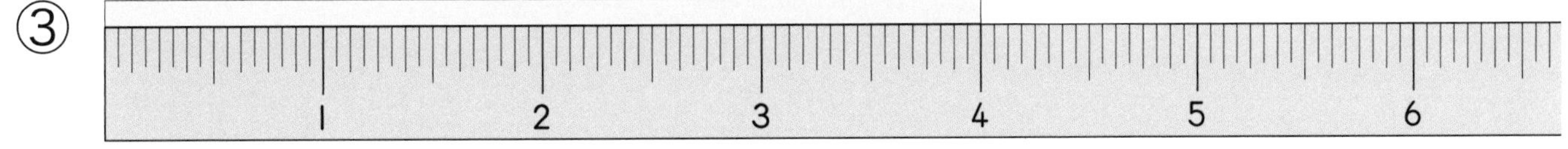

______ in.

④ 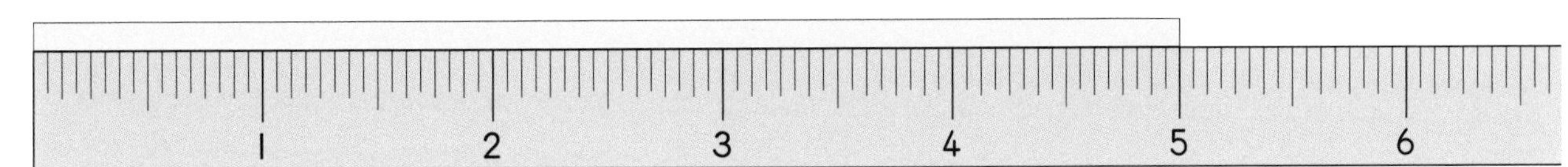

______ in.

⑤ 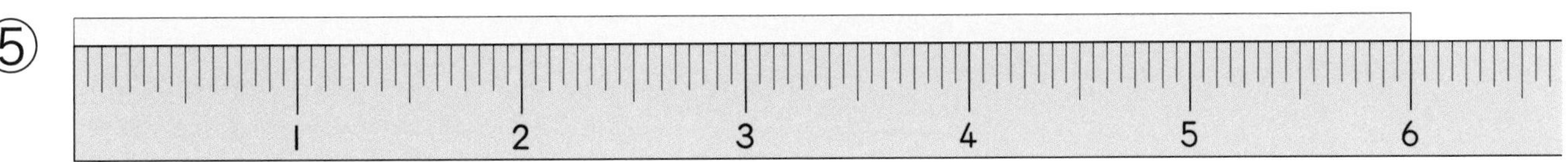

______ in.

■ How long is each yellow line? Answer in inches.

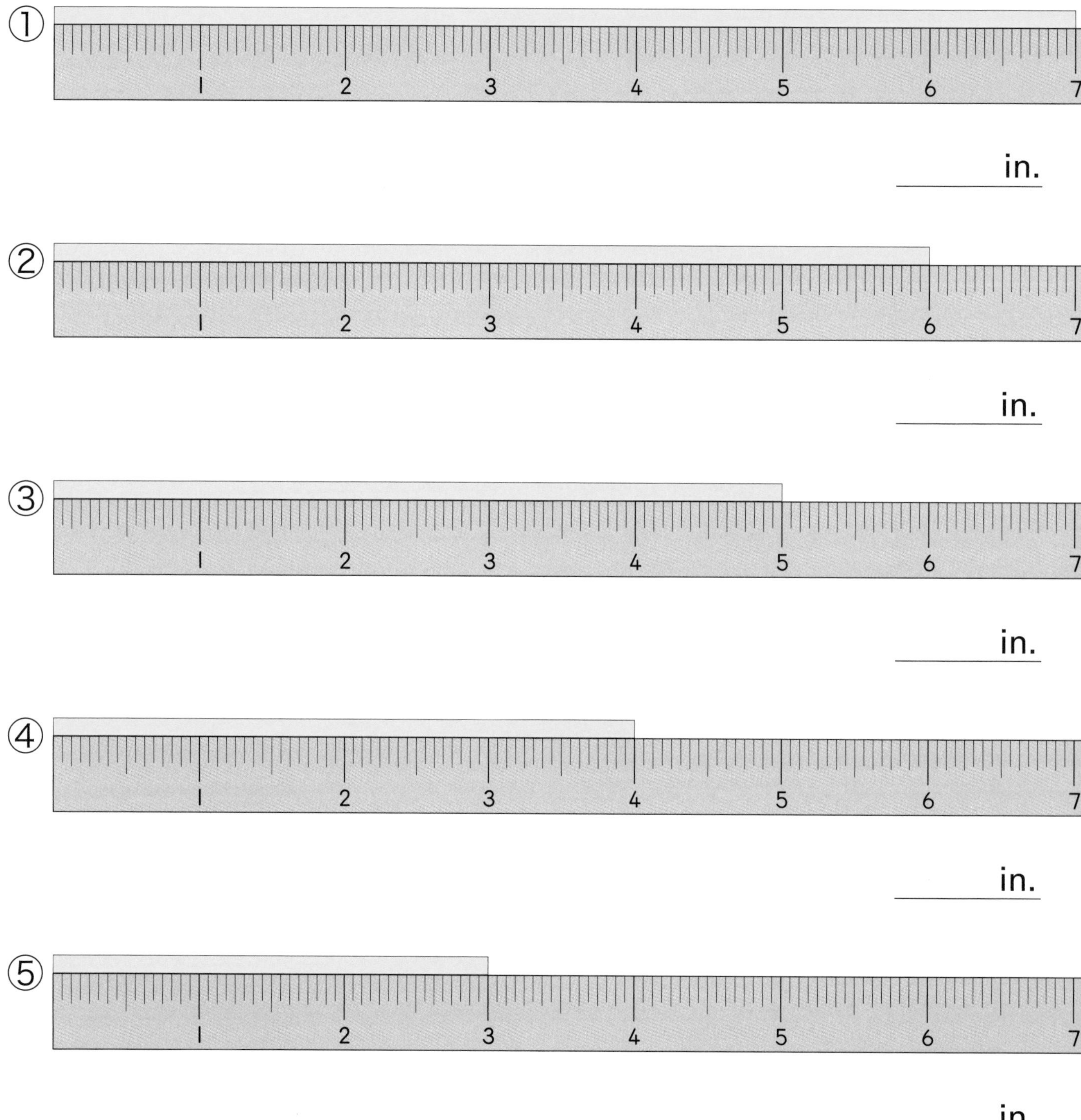

24 Measuring in Inches

Name

Date

■ How long is each yellow line? Answer in inches.

①
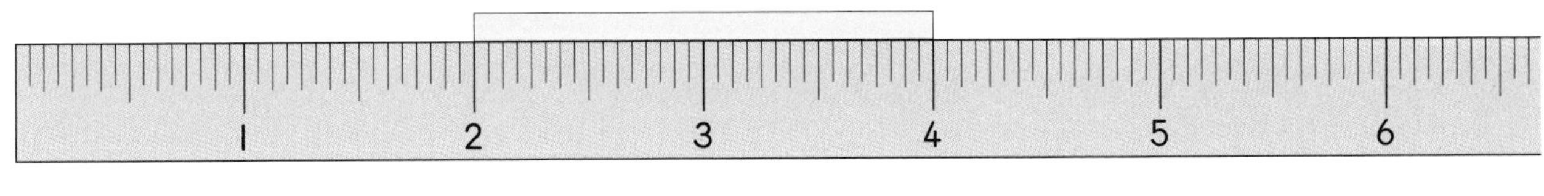

2 in.

②
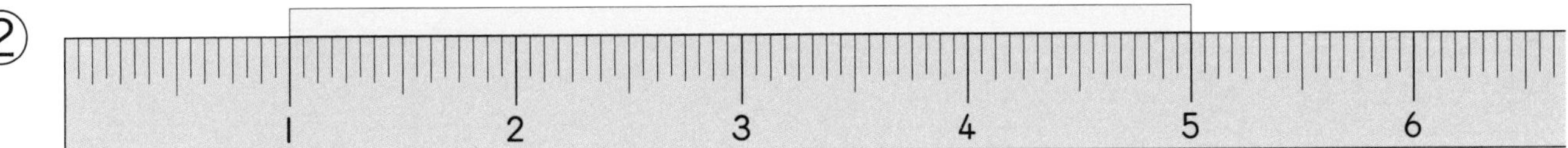

in.

③
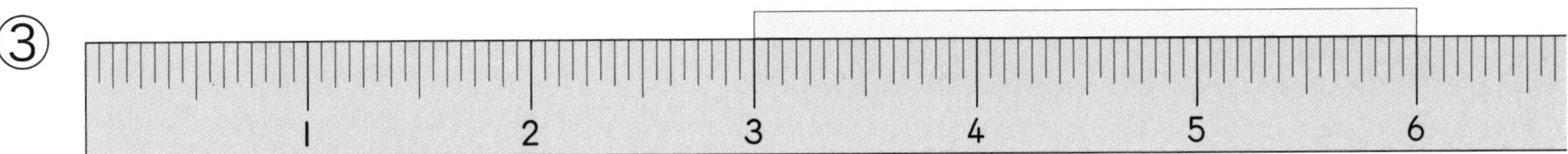

in.

④
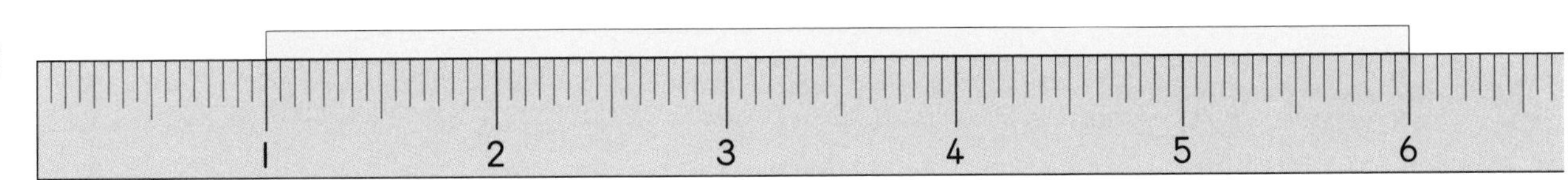

in.

⑤
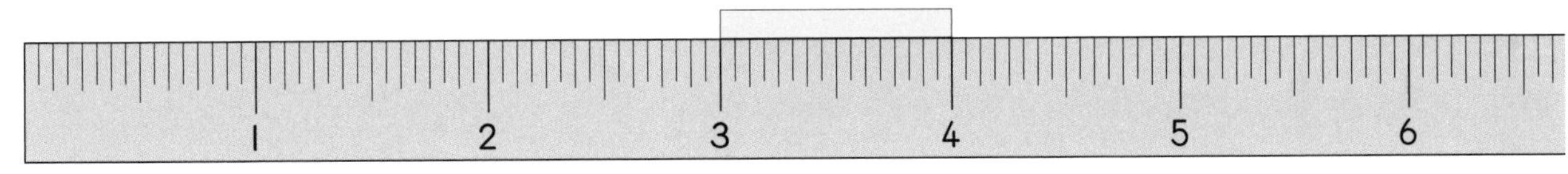

in.

■How long is each yellow line? Answer in inches.

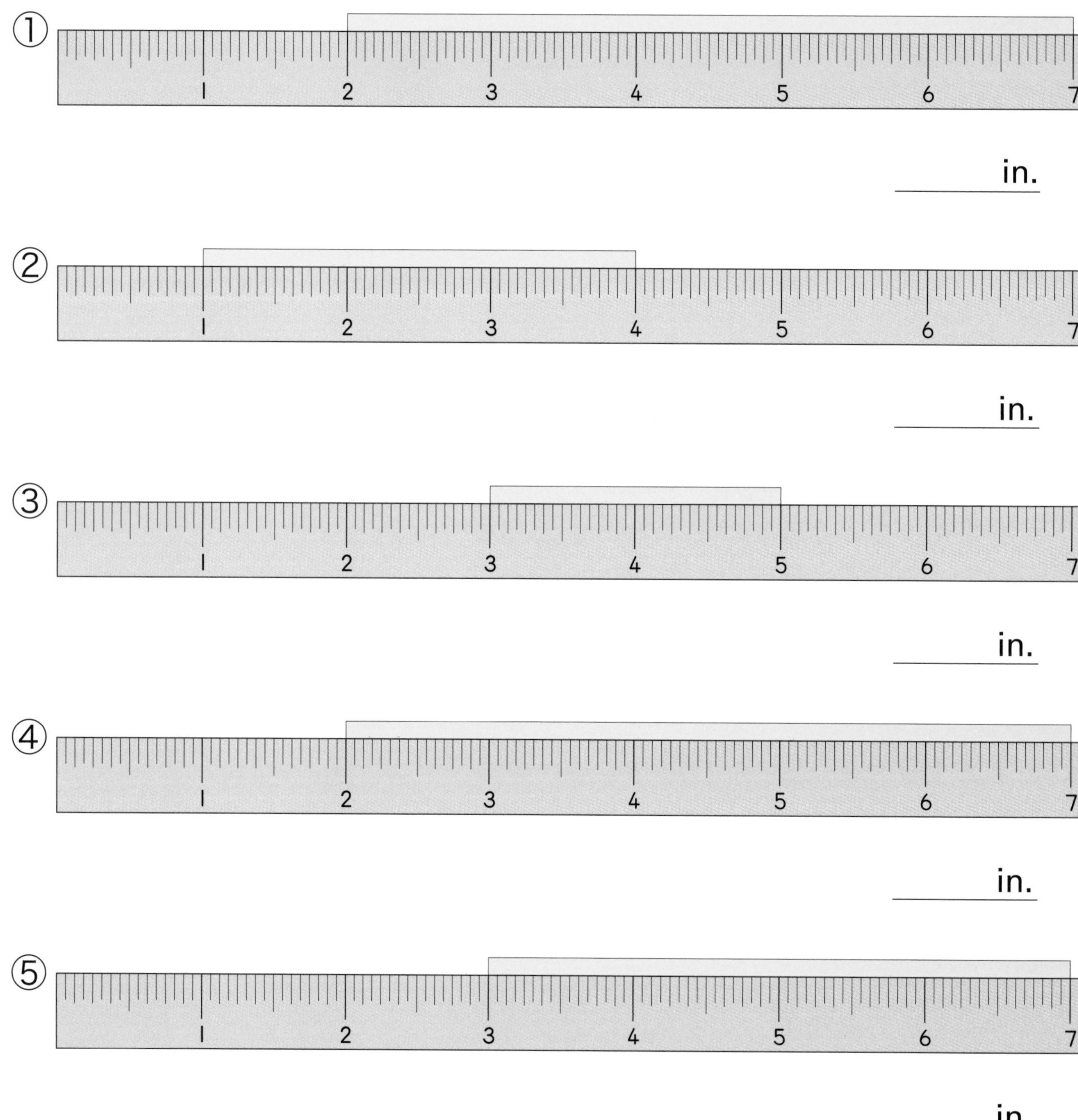

Measuring in Inches

Name

Date

To parents: When your child has completed this exercise, please check his or her answers with the Answer Key on the page 53.

■ How long is each bar? Use a ruler to answer in inches.

①

______ in.

②

______ in.

③

______ in.

④

______ in.

⑤

______ in.

To parents: When your child has completed this exercise, please check his or her answers with the Answer Key on the page 53.

■ How long is each bar? Use a ruler to answer in inches.

①

_____ in.

②

_____ in.

③

_____ in.

④

_____ in.

⑤

_____ in.

Measuring in Inches

Name

Date

To parents: When your child has completed this exercise, please check his or her answers with the Answer Key on the page 54.

■ How long is each bar? Use a ruler to answer in inches.

①

______ in.

②

______ in.

③

______ in.

④

______ in.

⑤

______ in.

To parents: When your child has completed this exercise, please check his or her answers with the Answer Key on the page 54.

■ How long is each bar? Use a ruler to answer in inches.

① ______ in.

② ______ in.

③ ______ in.

④ ______ in.

⑤ ______ in.

Review
Inches

Name

Date

■ Read the ruler from left to right. Fill in the missing numbers.

① 0 | 1 in. | ☐ in. | ☐ in.

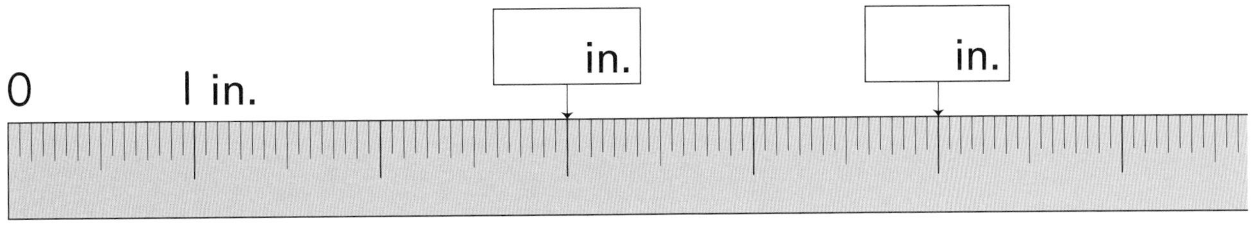

② 0 | 1 in. | ☐ in. | ☐ in.

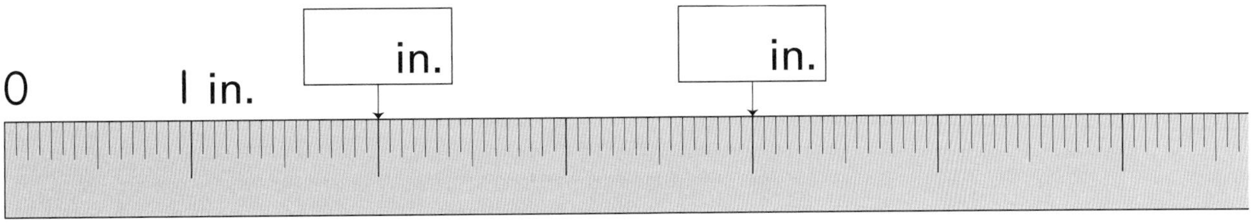

③ 0 | ☐ in. | ☐ in.

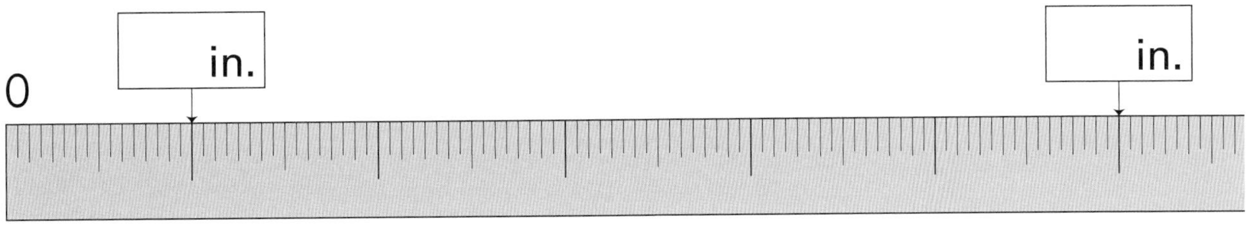

④ 6 in. | ☐ in. | ☐ in.

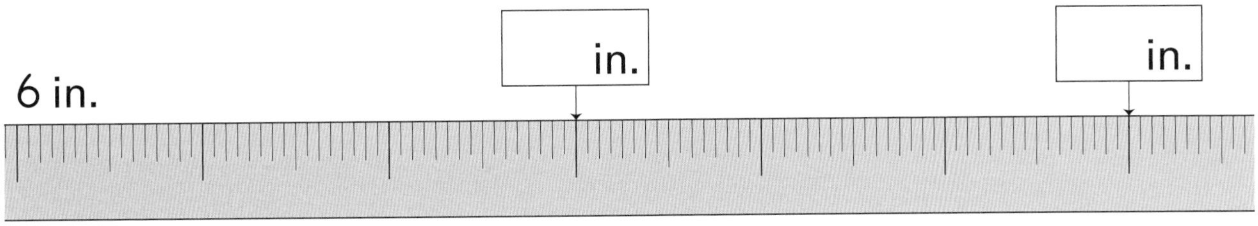

⑤ 6 in. | ☐ in. | ☐ in.

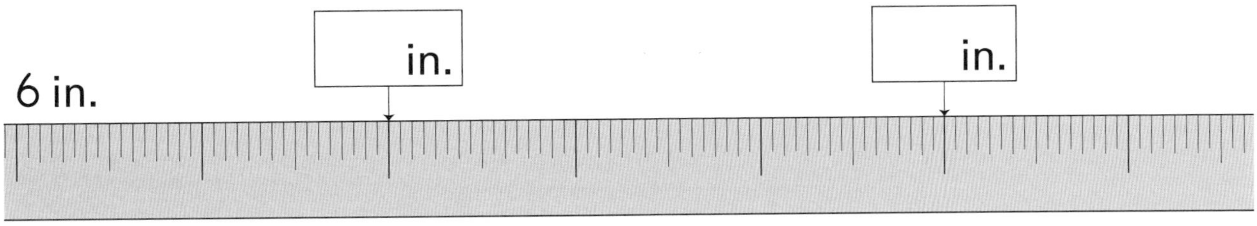

⑥ 6 in. | ☐ in. | ☐ in.

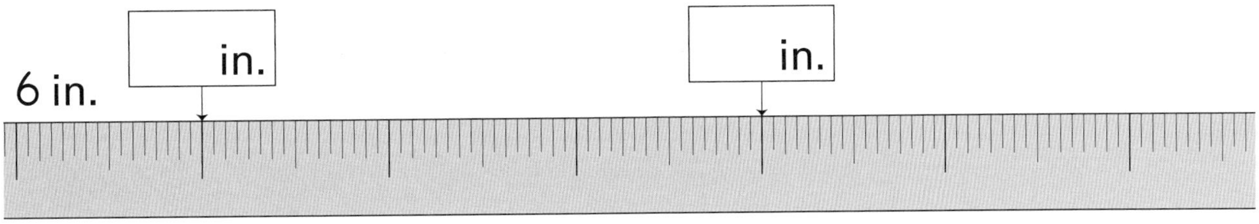

Answer Key P49 ① 1 in. ② 2 in. ③ 3 in. ④ 4 in. ⑤ 5 in.
P50 ① 6 in. ② 5 in. ③ 4 in. ④ 3 in. ⑤ 2 in.

■ How long is each yellow line? Answer in inches.

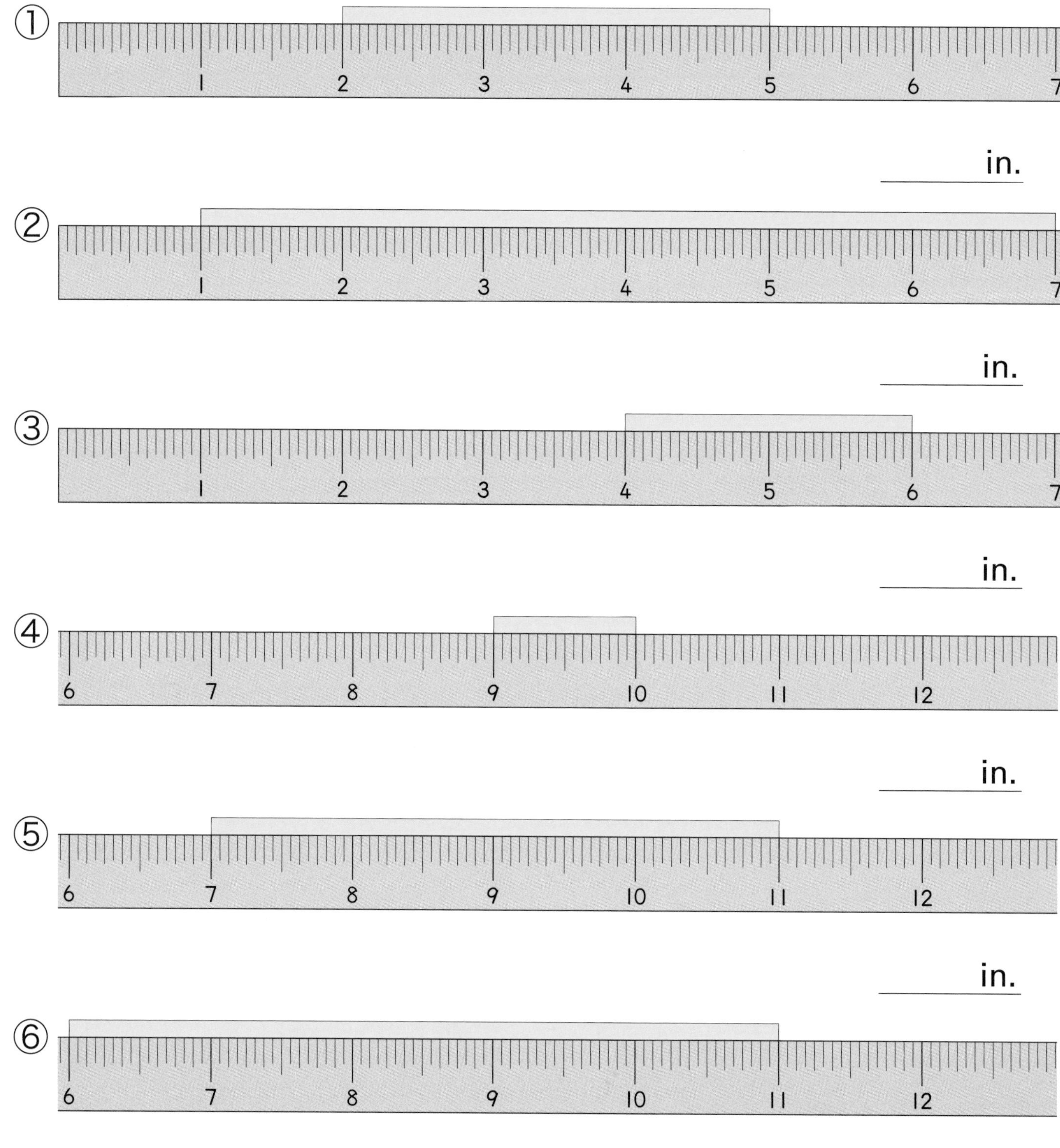

Answer Key P51 ① 3 in. ② 4 in. ③ 1 in. ④ 5 in. ⑤ 2 in.
P52 ① 4 in. ② 2 in. ③ 6 in. ④ 3 in. ⑤ 5 in.

28 Centimeters

Name

Date

■ Read the ruler from left to right. Fill in the missing number.

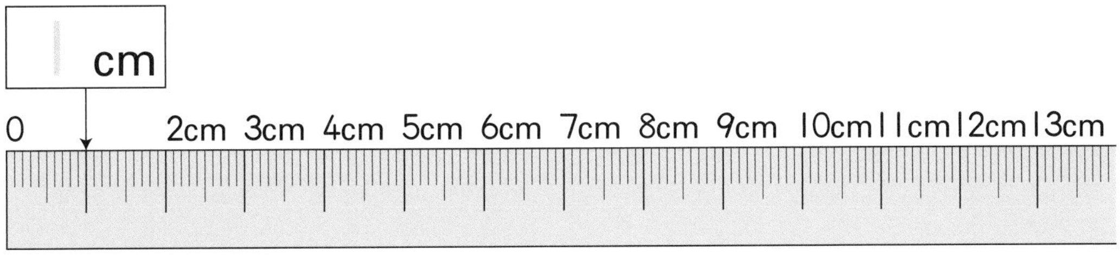

① [ ] cm
0 _ 2cm 3cm 4cm 5cm 6cm 7cm 8cm 9cm 10cm 11cm 12cm 13cm

② [ ] cm
0 1cm _ 3cm 4cm 5cm 6cm 7cm 8cm 9cm 10cm 11cm 12cm 13cm

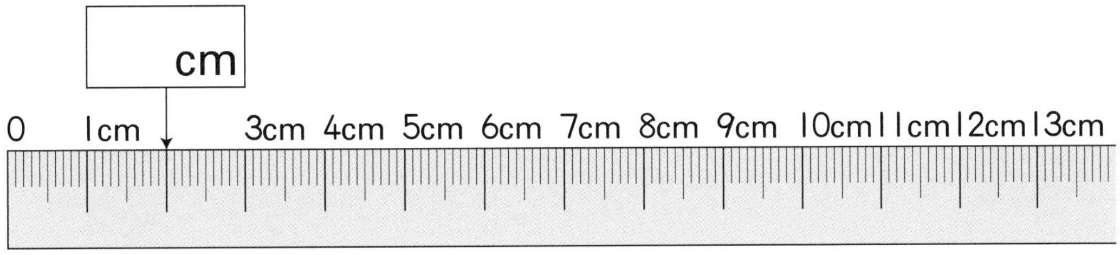

③ [ ] cm
0 1cm 2cm _ 4cm 5cm 6cm 7cm 8cm 9cm 10cm 11cm 12cm 13cm

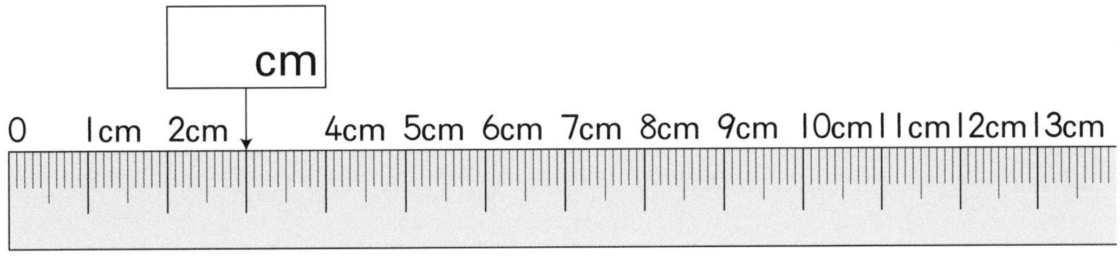

④ [ ] cm
0 1cm 2cm 3cm _ 5cm 6cm 7cm 8cm 9cm 10cm 11cm 12cm 13cm

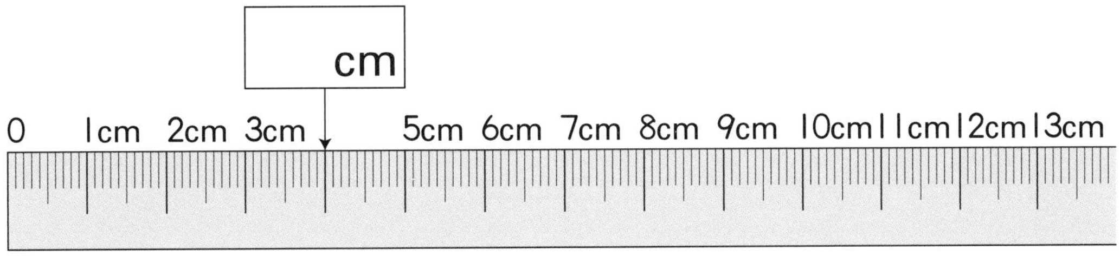

⑤ [ ] cm
0 1cm 2cm 3cm 4cm _ 6cm 7cm 8cm 9cm 10cm 11cm 12cm 13cm

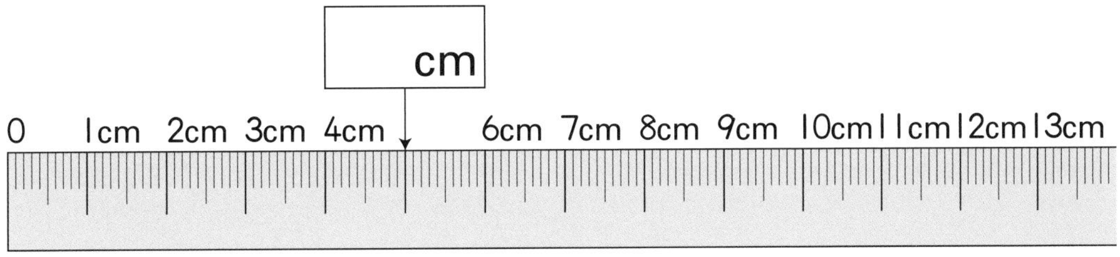

⑥ [ ] cm
0 1cm 2cm 3cm 4cm 5cm _ 7cm 8cm 9cm 10cm 11cm 12cm 13cm

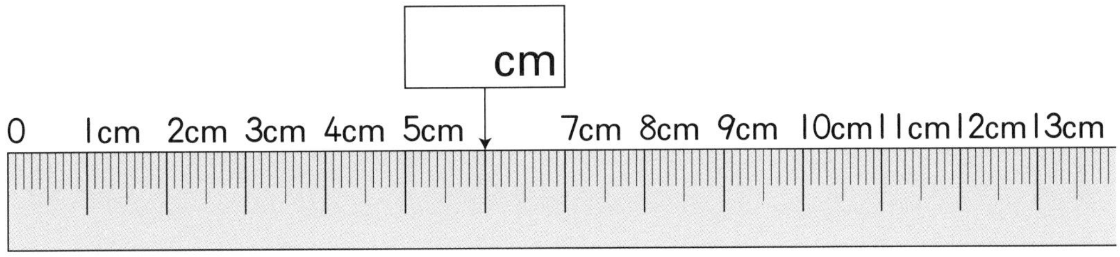

■ Read the ruler from left to right. Fill in the missing number.

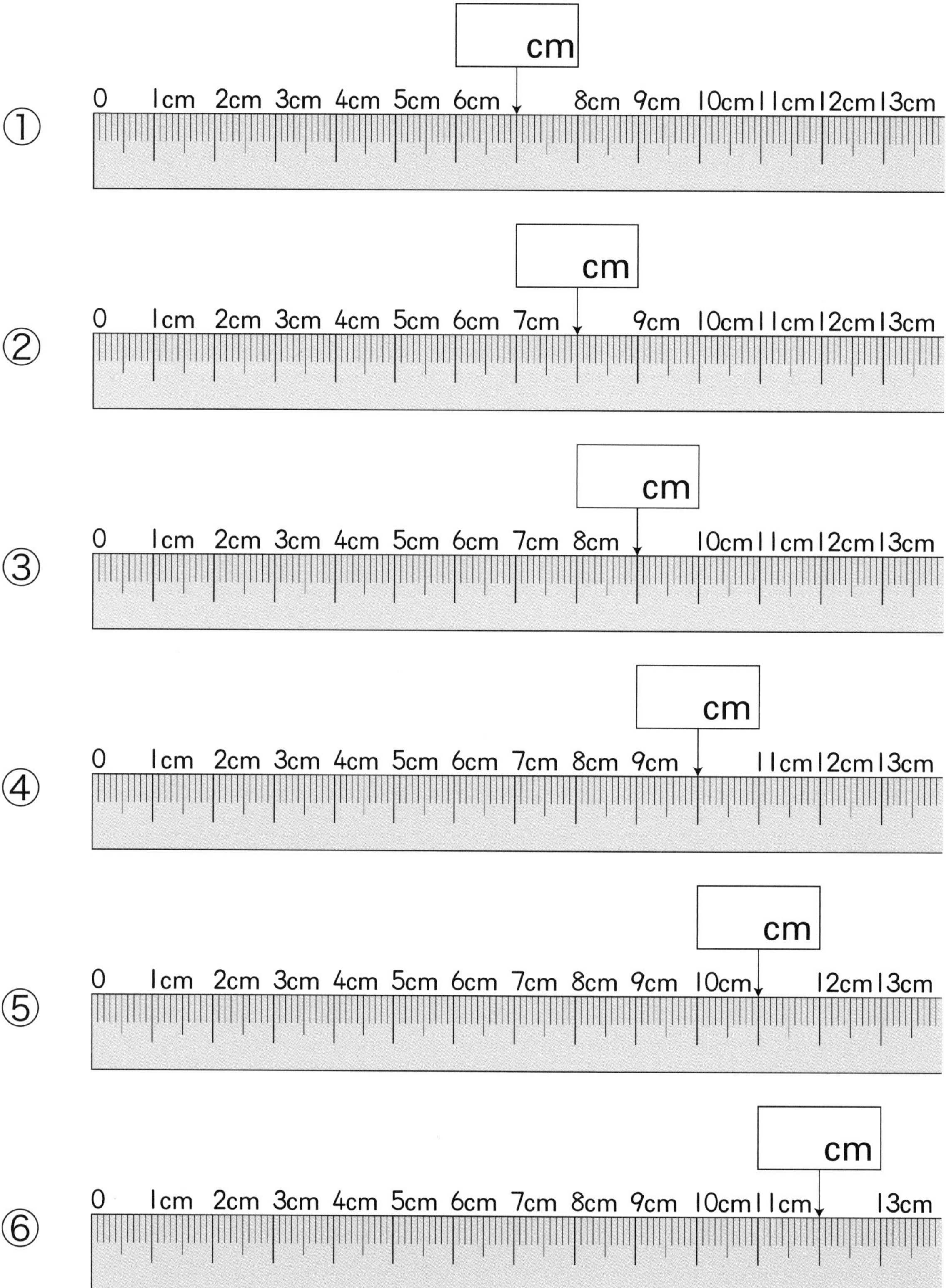

29 Centimeters

Name

Date

■ Read the ruler from left to right. Fill in the missing numbers.

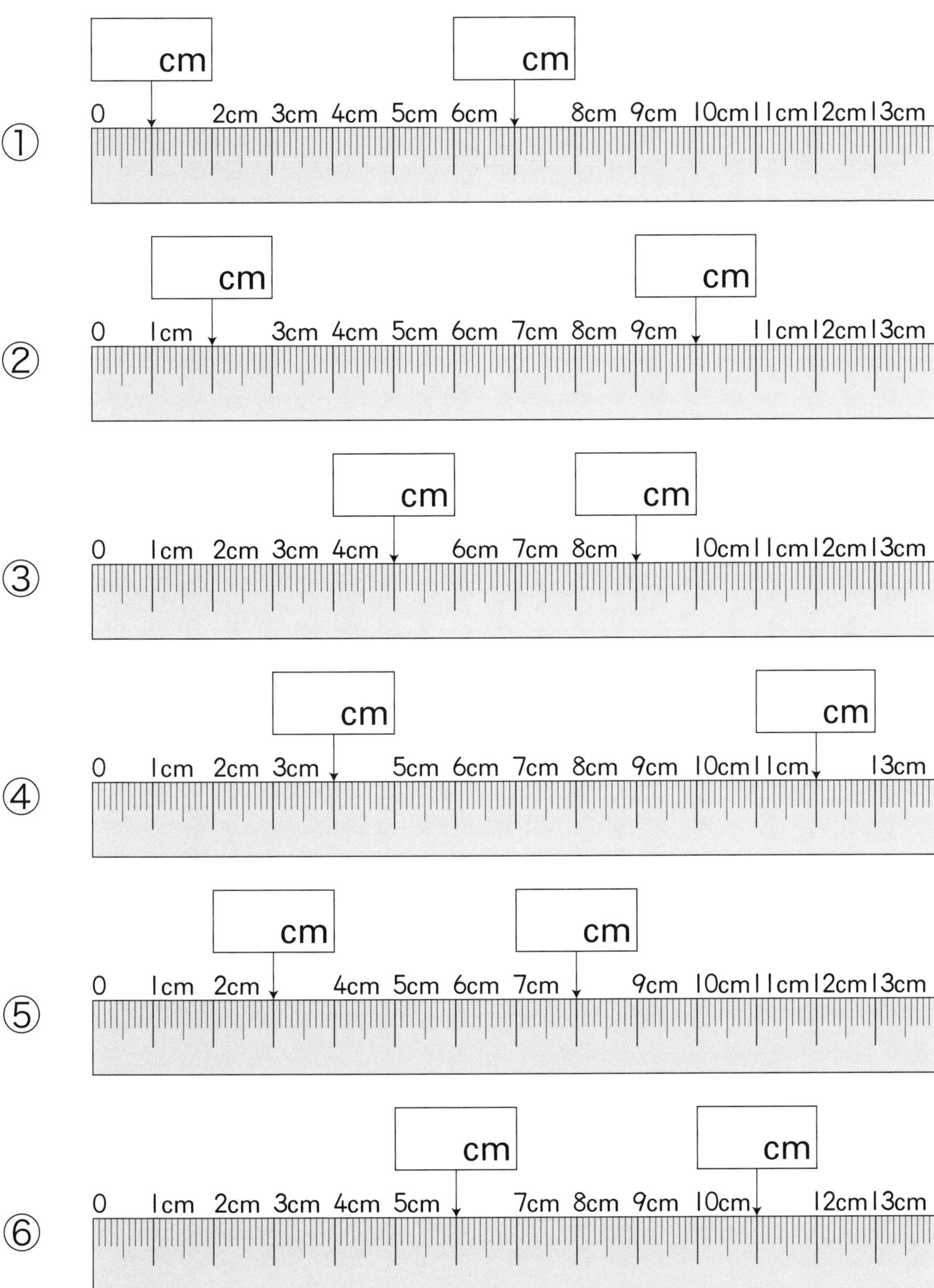

■ Read the ruler from left to right. Fill in the missing numbers.

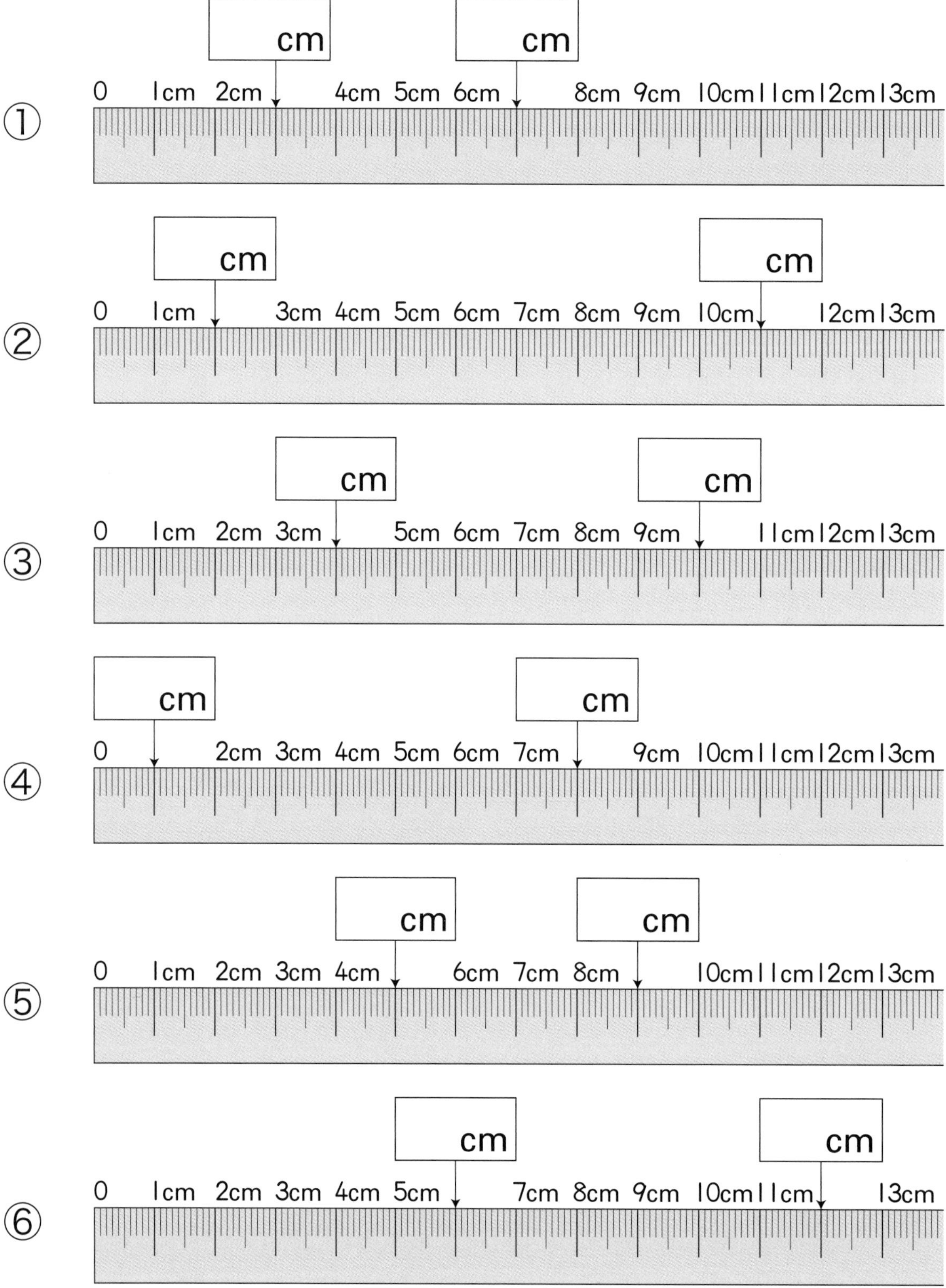

30 Centimeters

Name

Date

■ Read the ruler from left to right. Fill in the missing number.

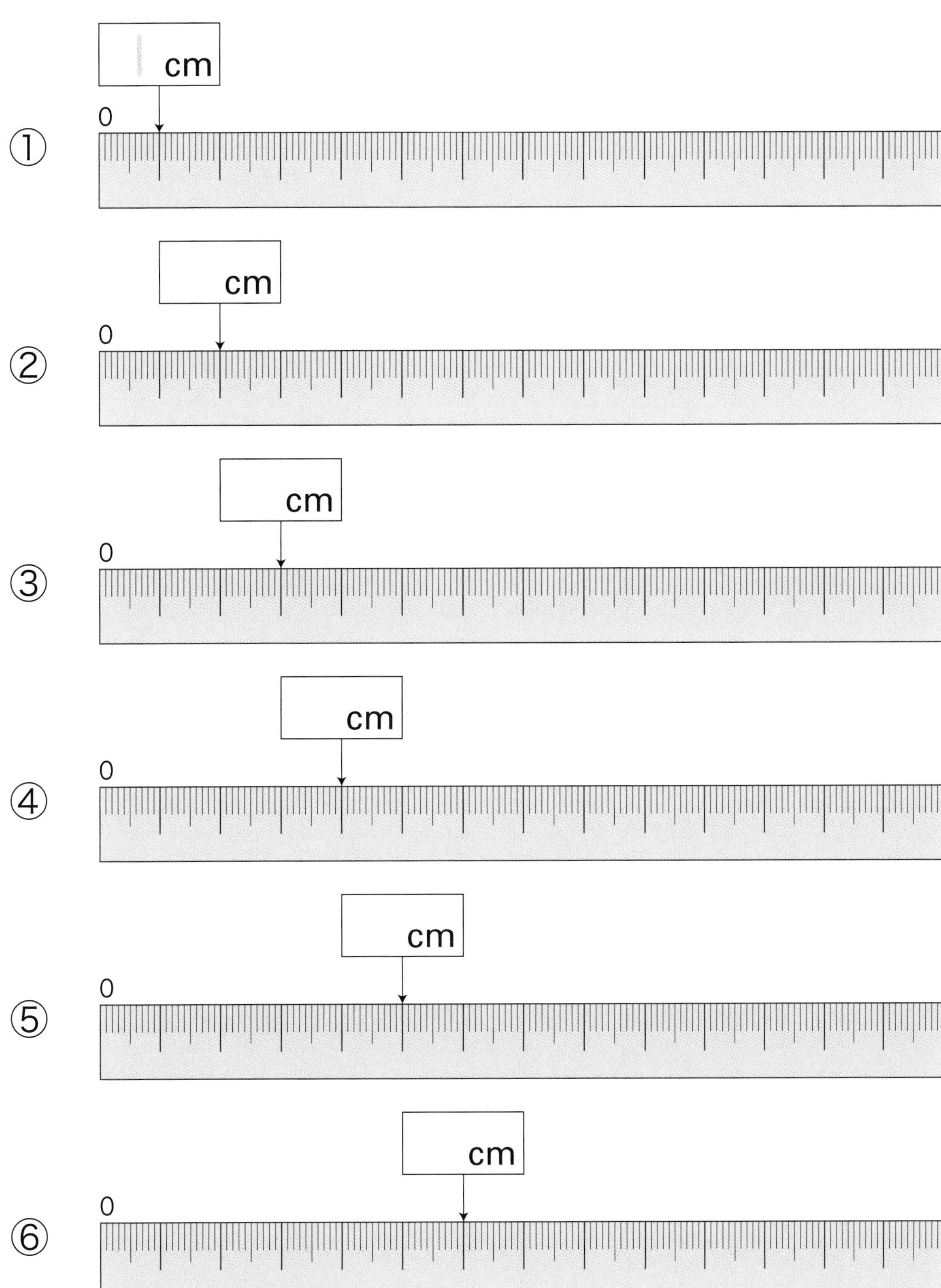

■Read the ruler from left to right. Fill in the missing number.

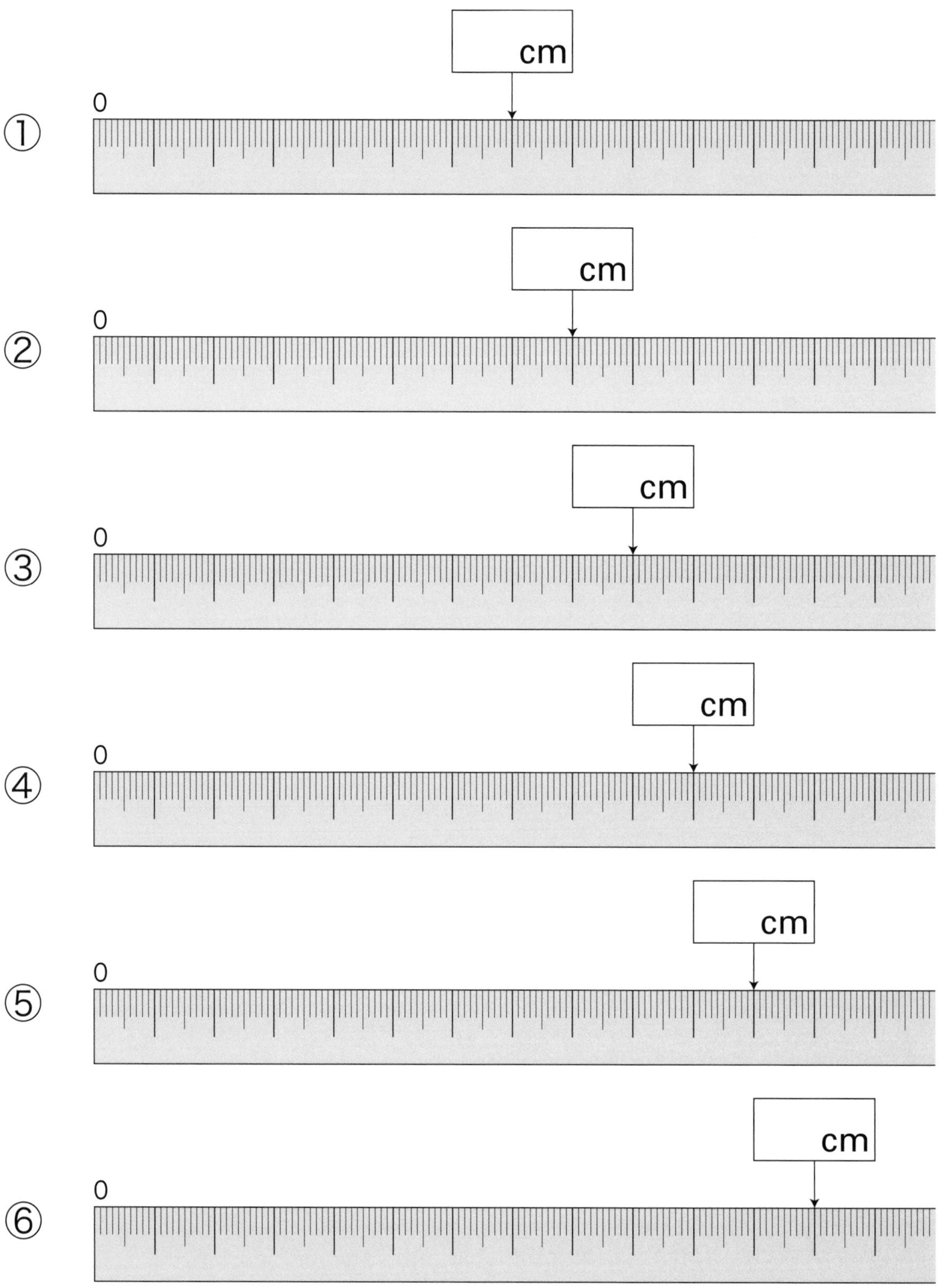

31 Centimeters

Name

Date

Read the ruler from left to right. Fill in the missing numbers.

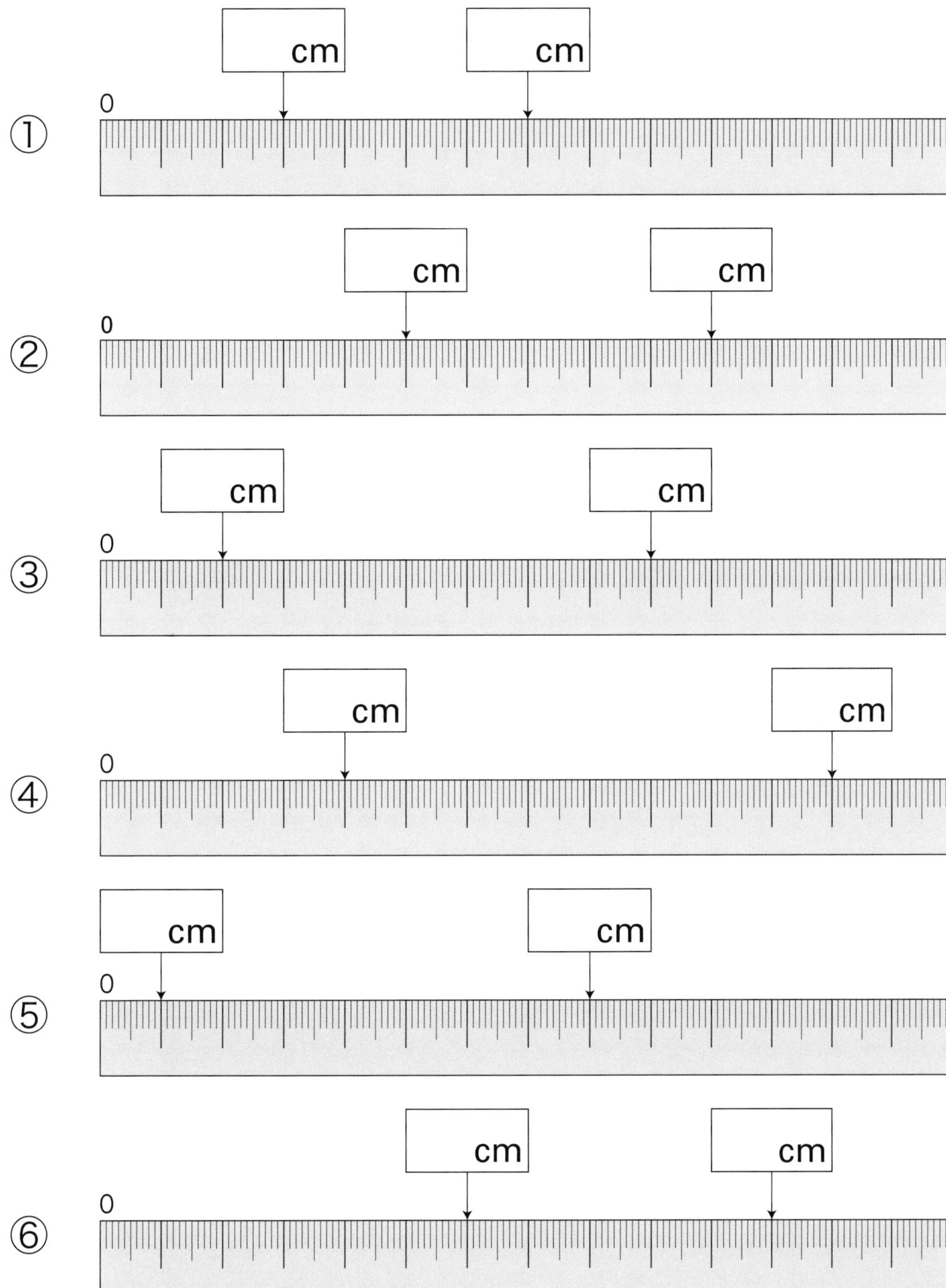

■Read the ruler from left to right. Fill in the missing numbers.

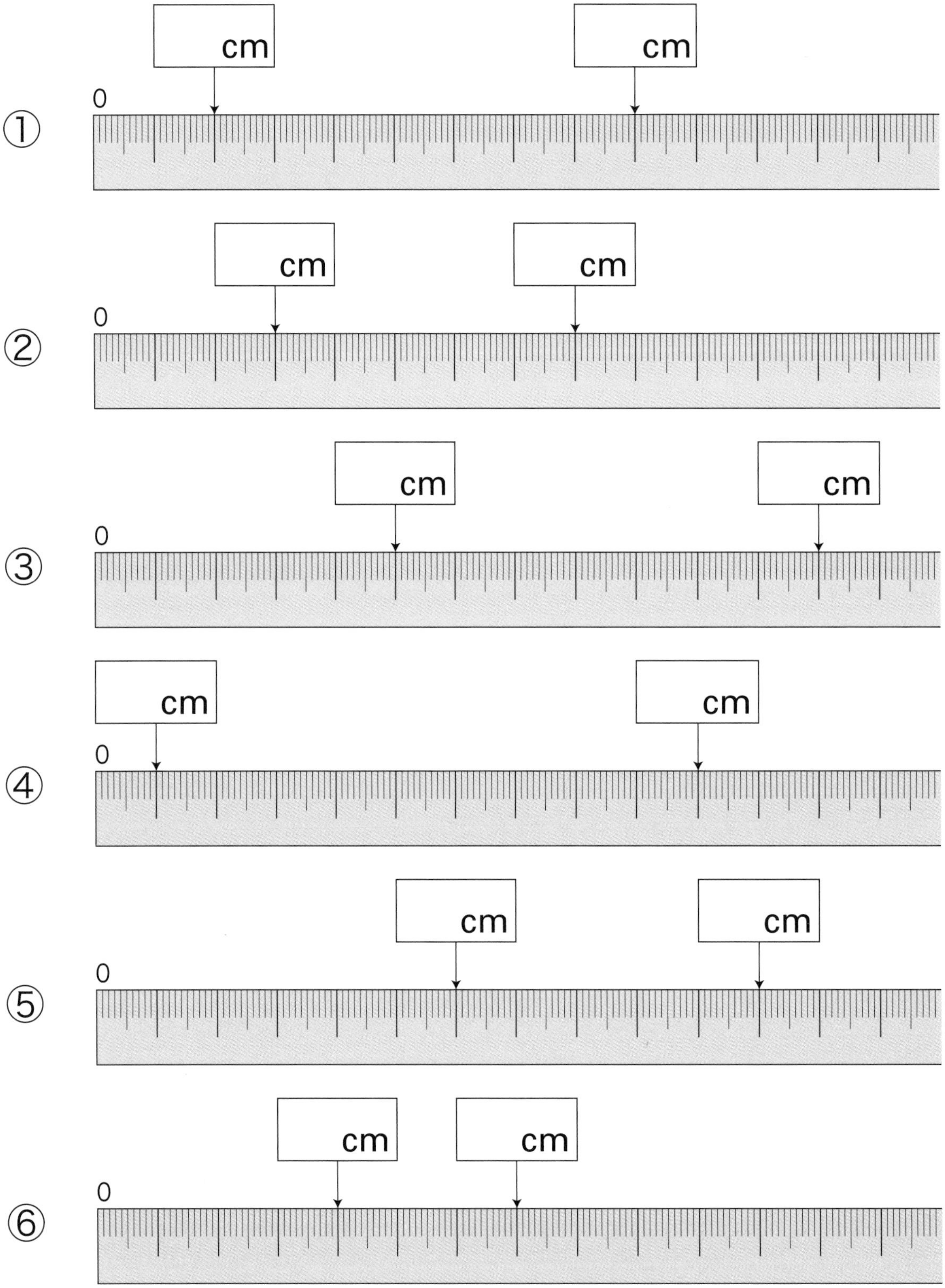

32 Measuring in Centimeters

Name
Date

■ How long is each red line? Answer in centimeters.

①

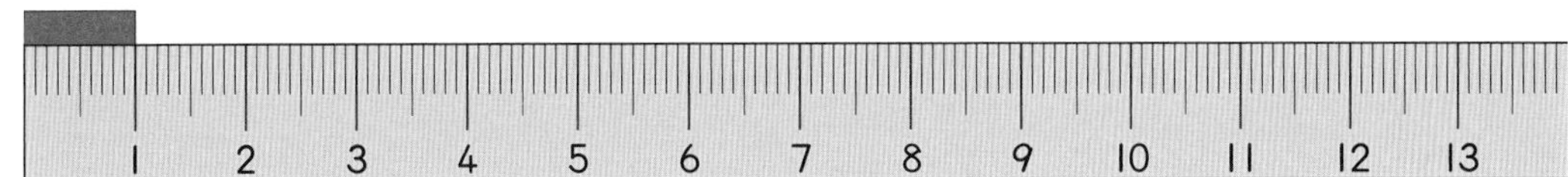

______ cm

②

______ cm

③

______ cm

④

______ cm

⑤

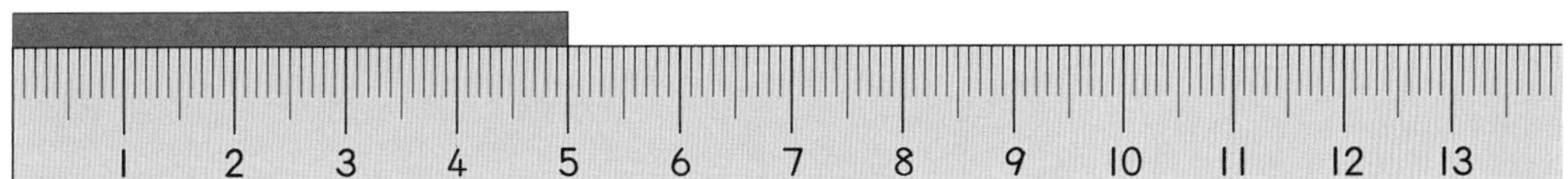

______ cm

⑥

______ cm

■How long is each red line? Answer in centimeters.

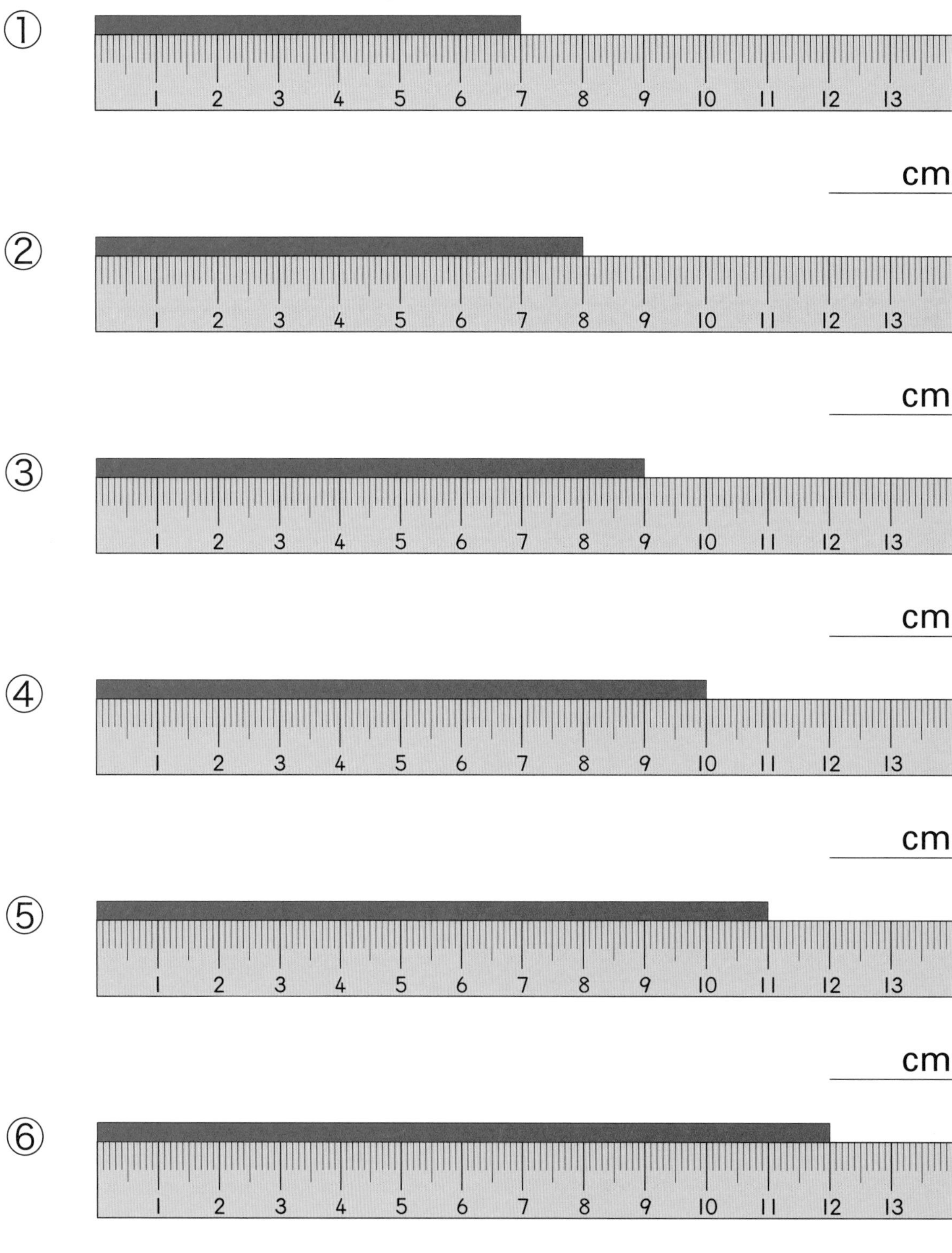

33 Measuring in Centimeters

Name

Date

How long is each red line? Answer in centimeters.

①

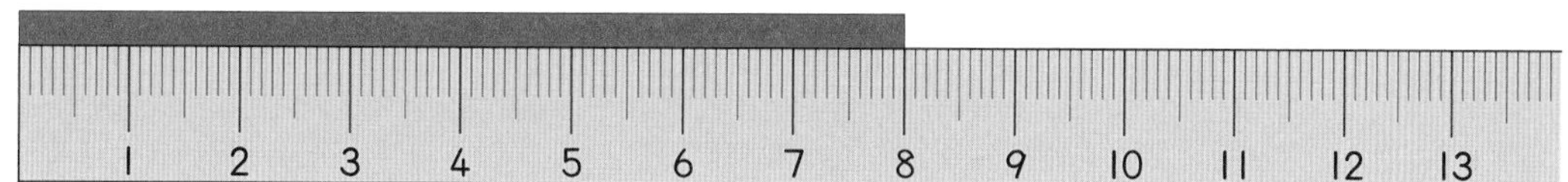

______ cm

②

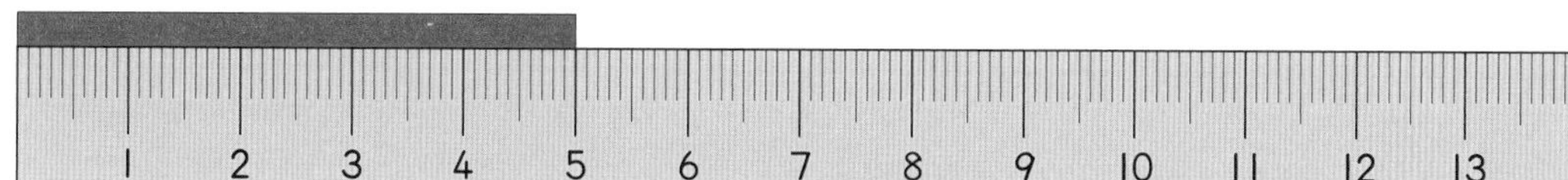

______ cm

③

______ cm

④

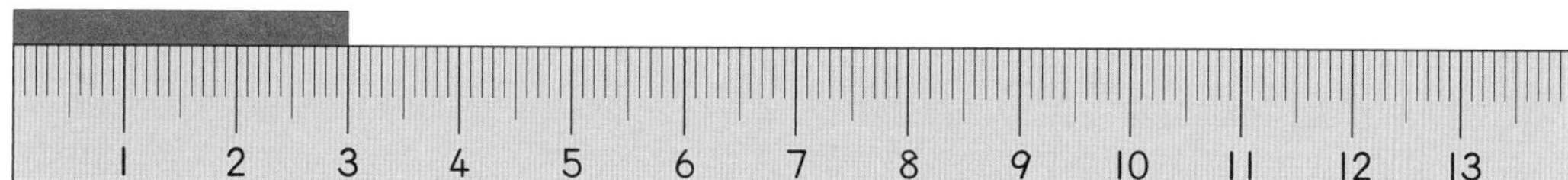

______ cm

⑤

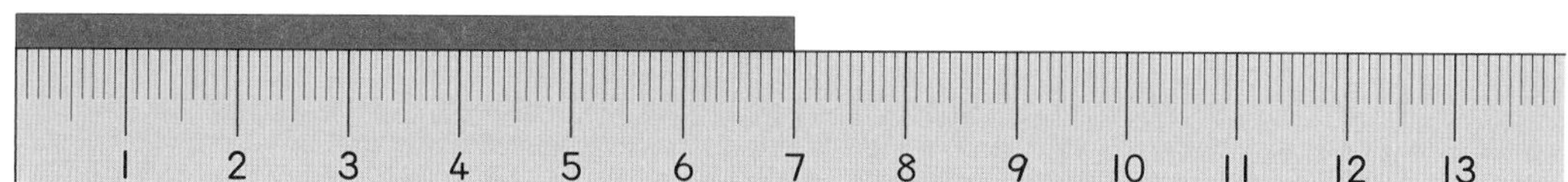

______ cm

⑥

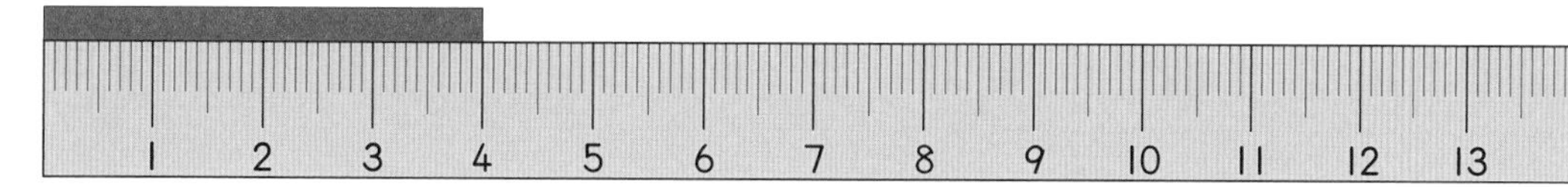

______ cm

■ How long is each red line? Answer in centimeters.

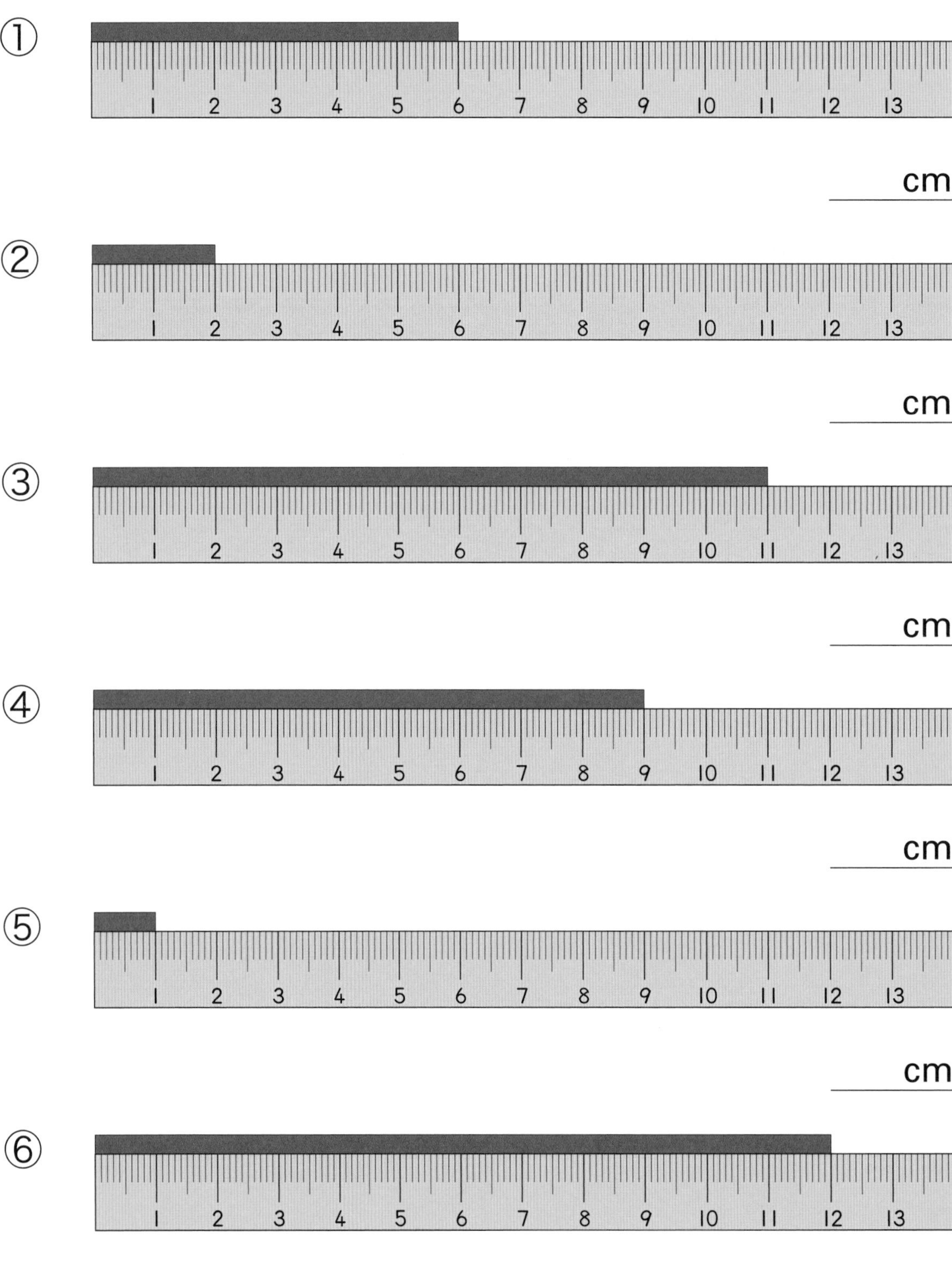

① ______ cm

② ______ cm

③ ______ cm

④ ______ cm

⑤ ______ cm

⑥ ______ cm

34 Measuring in Centimeters

Name

Date

■ How long is each red line? Answer in centimeters.

① 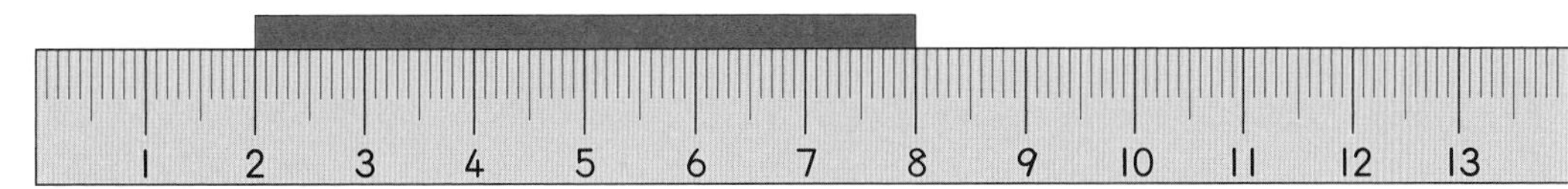

6 cm

② 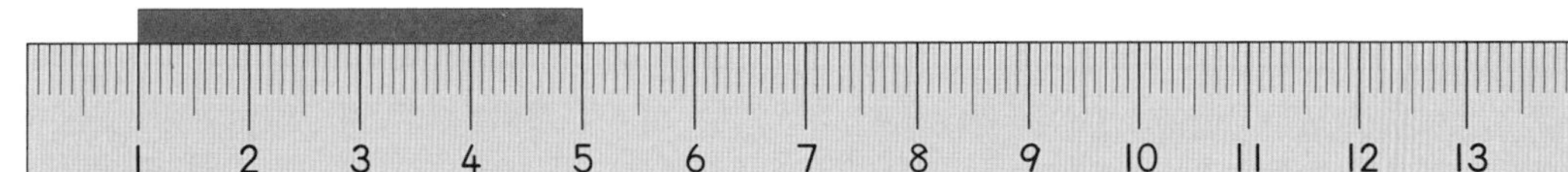

_____ cm

③ 

_____ cm

④ 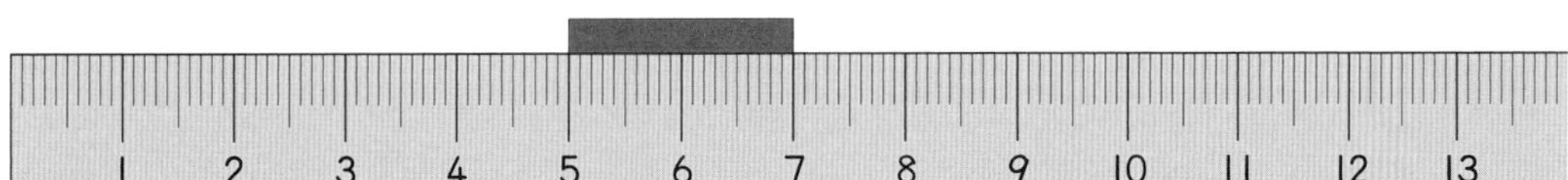

_____ cm

⑤ 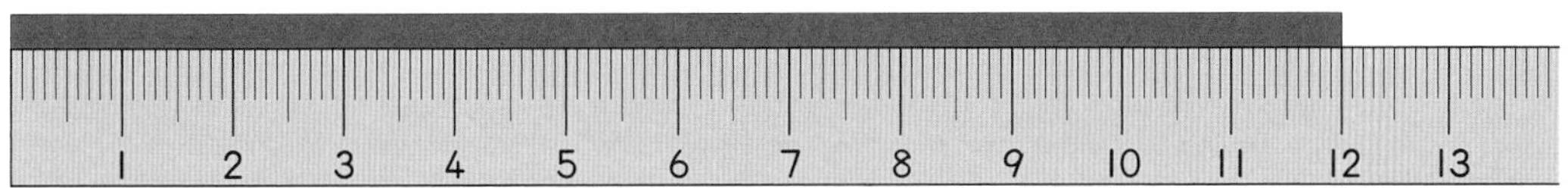

_____ cm

⑥ 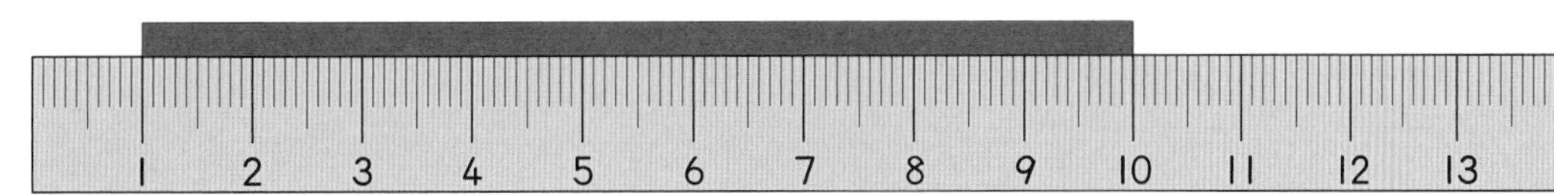

_____ cm

■How long is each red line? Answer in centimeters.

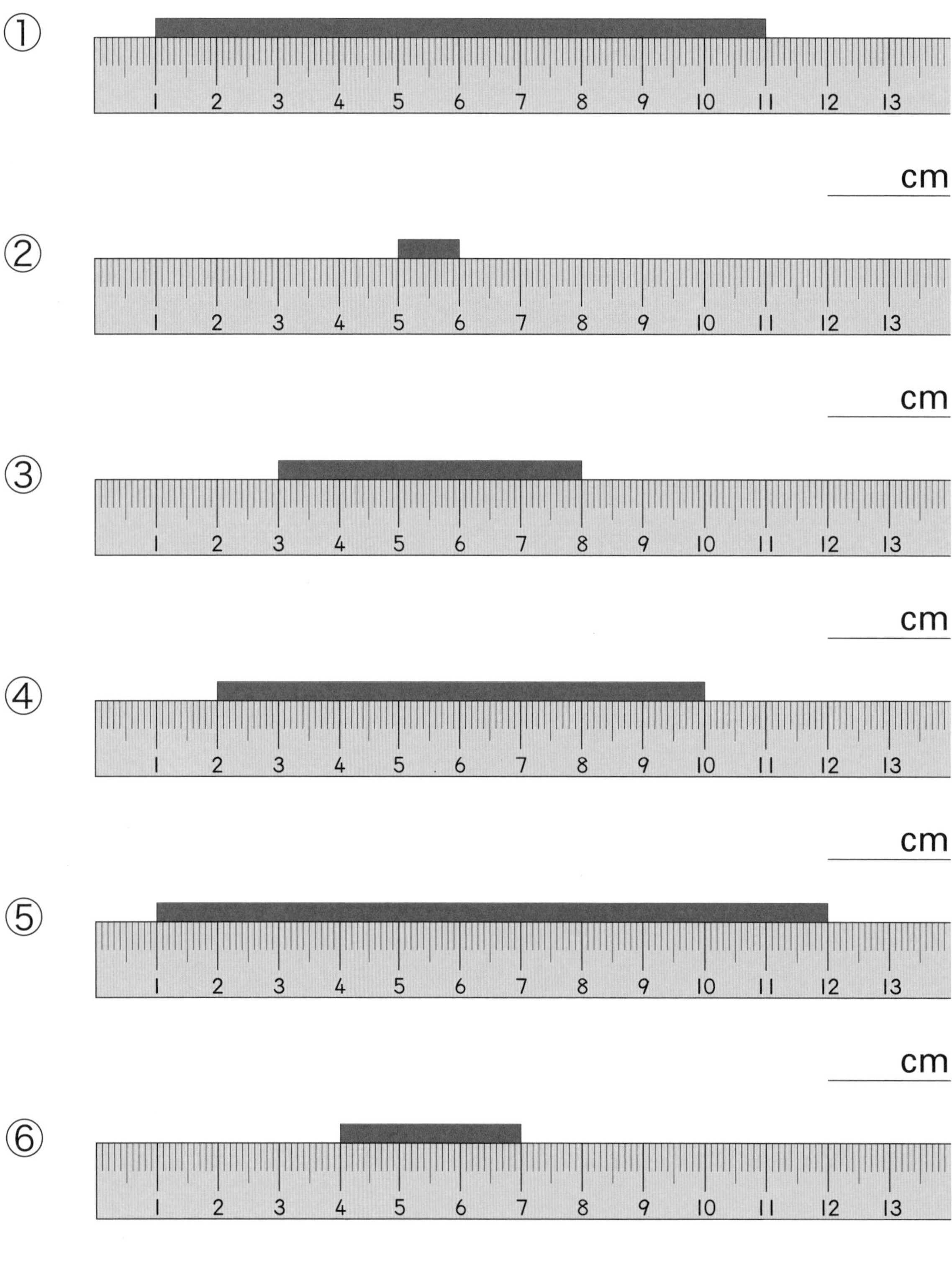

① ______ cm

② ______ cm

③ ______ cm

④ ______ cm

⑤ ______ cm

⑥ ______ cm

Measuring in Centimeters

Name

Date

To parents: When your child has completed this exercise, please check his or her answers with the Answer Key on the page 73.

■ How long is each bar? Use a ruler to answer in centimeters.

①

_____ cm

②

_____ cm

③

_____ cm

④

_____ cm

⑤

_____ cm

⑥

_____ cm

To parents: When your child has completed this exercise, please check his or her answers with the Answer Key on the page 73.

■ How long is each bar? Use a ruler to answer in centimeters.

①

______ cm

②

______ cm

③

______ cm

④

______ cm

⑤

______ cm

⑥

______ cm

Measuring in Centimeters

Name

Date

To parents: When your child has completed this exercise, please check his or her answers with the Answer Key on the page 74.

■ How long is each bar? Use a ruler to answer in centimeters.

① ______ cm

② ______ cm

③ ______ cm

④ ______ cm

⑤ ______ cm

⑥ ______ cm

To parents: When your child has completed this exercise, please check his or her answers with the Answer Key on the page 74.

■ How long is each bar? Use a ruler to answer in centimeters.

①

________ cm

②

________ cm

③

________ cm

④

________ cm

⑤

________ cm

⑥

________ cm

Review
Centimeters

Name

Date

■Read the ruler from left to right. Fill in the missing numbers.

① 0 — ☐ cm, ☐ cm

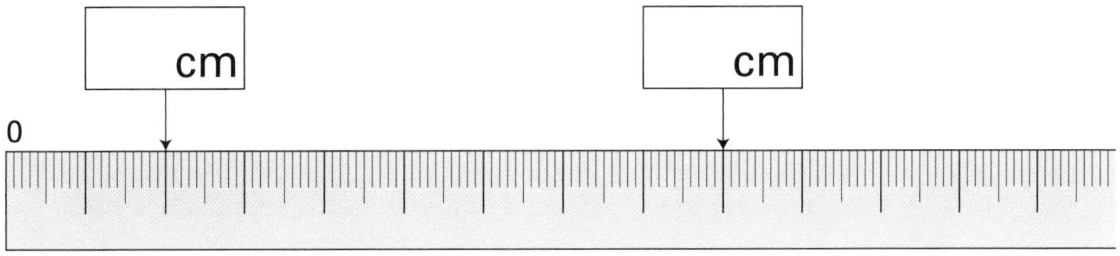

② 0 — ☐ cm, ☐ cm

③ 0 — ☐ cm, ☐ cm

④ 0 — ☐ cm, ☐ cm

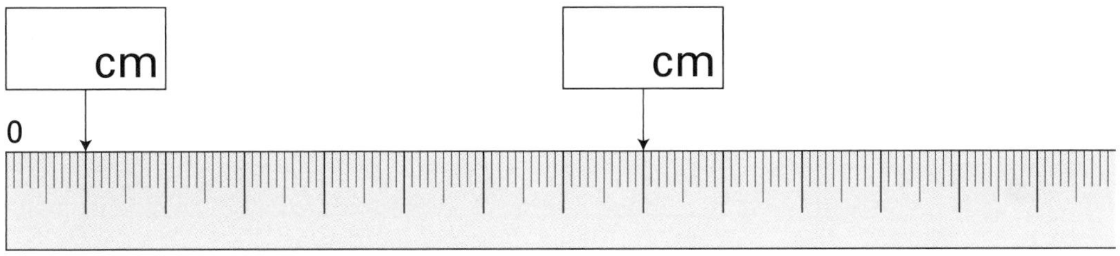

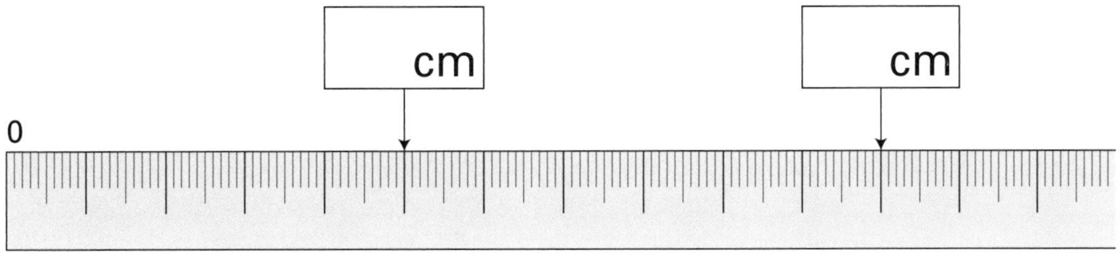

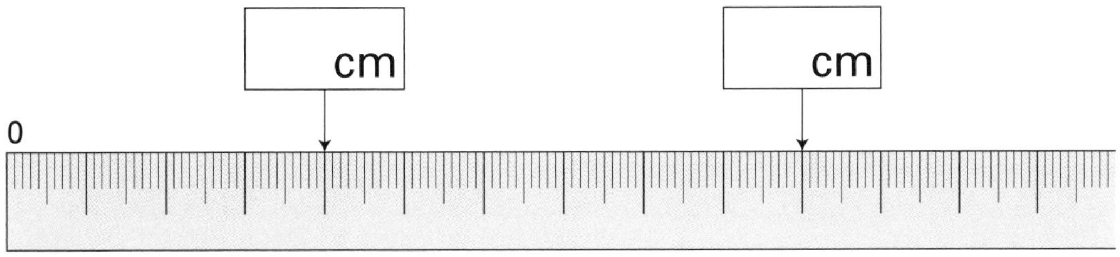

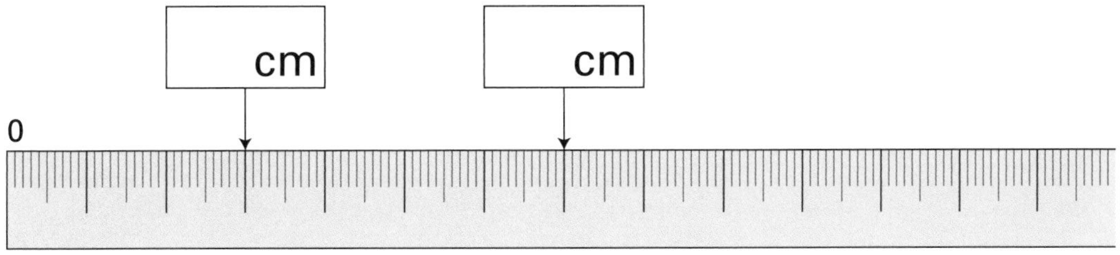

⑤ 0 — ☐ cm, ☐ cm

⑥ 0 — ☐ cm, ☐ cm

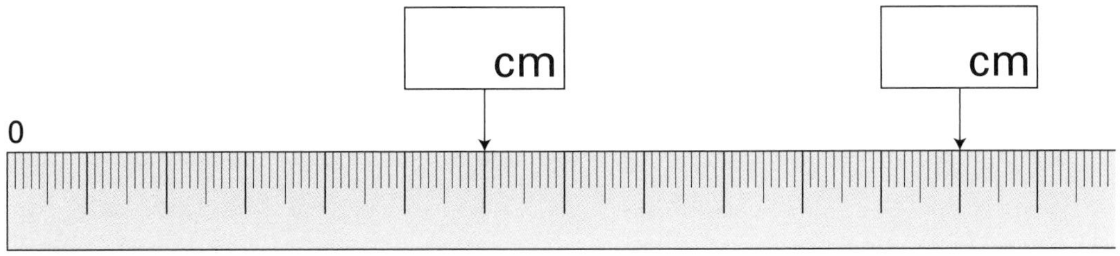

Answer Key P69 ① 1 cm ② 2 cm ③ 3 cm ④ 4 cm ⑤ 5 cm ⑥ 6 cm
P70 ① 7 cm ② 8 cm ③ 9 cm ④ 10cm ⑤ 11 cm ⑥ 12cm

■ How long is each red line? Answer in centimeters.

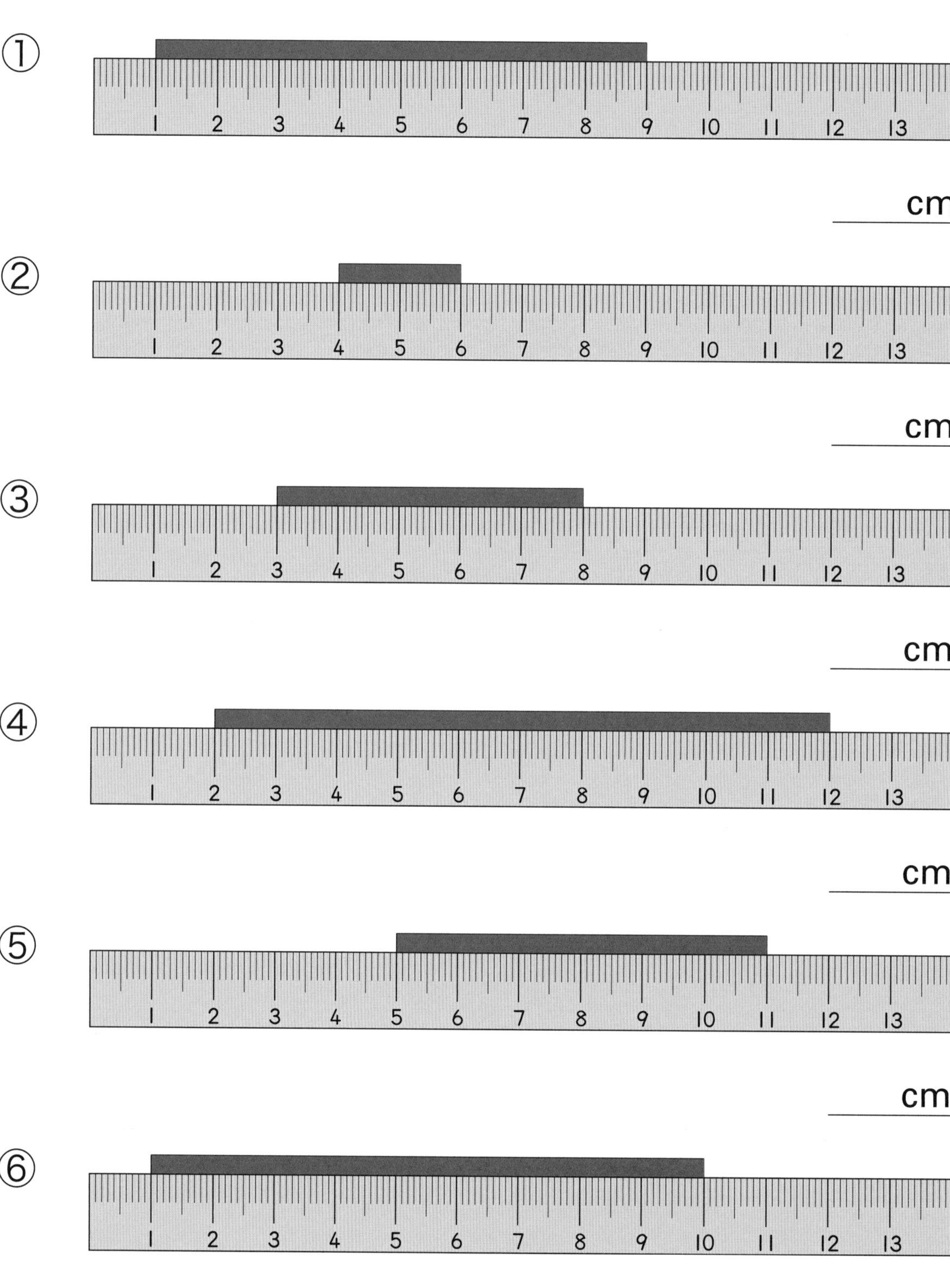

Answer Key P71 ① 5 cm ② 9 cm ③ 2 cm ④ 12cm ⑤ 3 cm ⑥ 8 cm
P72 ① 10cm ② 6 cm ③ 4 cm ④ 7 cm ⑤ 11 cm ⑥ 1 cm

Review

Name
Date

To parents: When your child has completed this exercise, please check his or her answers with the Answer Key on the page 76.

■ How long is each bar? Use a ruler to answer in inches.

① ______ in.

② ______ in.

③ ______ in.

④ ______ in.

⑤ ______ in.

⑥ ______ in.

Answer Key P76 ① 4 cm ② 8 cm ③ 3 cm ④ 11 cm ⑤ 10 cm ⑥ 6 cm

To parents: When your child has completed this exercise, please check his or her answers with the Answer Key on the page 75.

■ How long is each bar? Use a ruler to answer in centimeters.

①

______ cm

②

______ cm

③

______ cm

④

______ cm

⑤

______ cm

⑥

______ cm

Answer Key P75 ① 2 in. ② 5 in. ③ 4 in. ④ 1 in. ⑤ 6 in. ⑥ 3 in.

KUMON

Certificate of Achievement

____

is hereby congratulated on completing

My Book of Measurement: Length

Presented on ______________________, 20___

____

Parent or Guardian